THE IRISH EXPERIMENT

Zach Tuohy's remarkable journey from Gaelic football in Ireland to becoming one of the most successful Irish imports in the Australian Football League (AFL) is a tale of determination, adaptability and sheer talent. A standout athlete from a young age, Tuohy was recruited by Carlton at the age of 19. After seven years at Carlton, he joined Geelong, where he clinched a Premiership in 2022 and became a fan favourite. Celebrated for his resilience and excellence, Tuohy has played a record-breaking number of games for an Irish player and stands as a towering figure in AFL history. As Tuohy celebrates an impressive 15th year in the AFL in 2024, his life off the field is equally fulfilling. Residing in Geelong with his wife and two sons, he embodies the spirit of dedication and community.

Catherine Murphy started her career in the sports department of RTÉ, Ireland's national broadcaster, before moving to Australia in 2006 to work with Fox Sports. In 2018, Catherine joined ABC, where she works as a sports presenter on TV and radio. She also hosts podcasts.

The Irish Experiment is her first book.

THE IRISH EXPERIMENT
From the GAA to the AFL

Zach Tuohy
with Catherine Murphy

HACHETTE
BOOKS
IRELAND

First published in Ireland in 2024 by
HACHETTE BOOKS IRELAND

1

Cataloguing in Publication Data is available from the British Library.

The line of poetry from 'Good Timber' by Douglas Malloch has
been reproduced with kind permission from bible.org.

Photograph credits: © INPHO/Cathal Noonan, p2 (top left); courtesy
of AFL: p2 (bottom), p3 (bottom), p4 (bottom), p5, 6 (top), p8 (top).

ISBN 9781399738736

Typeset in Sabon by Bookends Publishing Services, Dublin
Printed and bound in Great Britain by Clays Ltd, Elcograf S.p.A.

Hachette Books Ireland policy is to use papers that are natural, renewable
and recyclable products and made from wood grown in sustainable
forests. The logging and manufacturing processes are expected to
conform to the environmental regulations of the country of origin.

Hachette Books Ireland
8 Castlecourt Centre
Castleknock
Dublin 15, Ireland

A division of Hachette UK Ltd
Carmelite House, 50 Victoria Embankment, London EC4Y 0DZ

www.hachettebooksireland.ie

To my boys, Flynn and Rafferty

Contents

CHAPTER 1

Prisoners and Patients

MY OLD MAN SPENT A LOT OF TIME IN PRISON.

Sorry, let me rephrase that.

My father worked as a prison officer in Portlaoise prison, a maximum-security facility, for 30 years.

A lot of people say the prison is what Portlaoise is best known for, along with the Midlands Regional Hospital. The hospital was opened in the 1930s, while the prison started operating in the 1830s, making it one of Ireland's oldest-running prisons. There are generations of families back home who have known only the prison and the hospital as their employers. These two institutions are the bedrock of our town. And we are rightly proud of that.

Portlaoise is a small town in the south midlands. I think of it as being right in the heart of Ireland, but I'm biased. Growing up, it felt like a metropolitan city to me. When I picture myself at home, I think of walking up the main street in Portlaoise on its cobblestone paths, flanked on either side by pubs, cafés and shops.

Smack bang in the middle of main street is the courthouse where, on any given Tuesday, you might see, on the steps, some of Ireland's more colourful characters, waiting with family to find out if they or their loved ones would be spending the foreseeable future in the nearby prison.

People may say Portlaoise is best known for its prison, but I say we're known best for our Gaelic football club. Nicknamed 'The Town' (words that you may have seen on the flag I brought on stage during the AFL Premiership medal presentation), it is central to everything that happens in the community. All my childhood and teenage memories revolve around one place – the GAA (Gaelic Athletic Association) club.

When I think of the club, I think of the white pebble-dashed clubhouse with five change rooms to facilitate all age groups in both men's and women's football and hurling/camogie (the women's version of hurling) and an indoor hall for presentation nights – and, more importantly, to host teenage discos where I would go to work my magic on the ladies. And when I say 'work my magic', I mean stand nervously, alone in the corner, absolutely refusing to approach or even make eye contact with a girl.

The club now boasts a well-equipped gym, with a picture of someone you know on the wall, who, at the time the photo was taken, was celebrating an AFL Grand Final. But we'll talk about that much later.

We also had a club bar, where we would gather after games and eat Tayto crisps (iconic Irish crisps) and consume as many soft drinks as we could muster while the parents had a pint. Bliss.

Family, friends, golf, snooker, hurling, soccer and football – that's what I think of when I think of Portlaoise.

I love it. I absolutely fucking love Portlaoise.

That's why leaving was so hard.

My father grew up in Portlaoise too. He always says he married for love and that he joined the prison service for his kids. My mother, Marie, and my father, Noel, met on 19 December 1975 and were married on 26 January 1980. Their marraige produced four kids and our neighbouring prison offered the stability necessary to provide for those kids. Mammy and Daddy had my sister Naomi in 1981, followed by Noel John in 1983, Hannah in 1987, then me, the youngest, born on 10 December 1989.

My old man was one of 10 children – six boys and four girls. A big Irish family, and a happy one. They were certainly not born with a silver spoon in their mouths but that hardly mattered. My granny was a wonderful mother, who made sure her kids had everything they needed.

Like his mother before him, Daddy's goal in life was to ensure his children had an even better life than he had. His career was all about us.

I often think about how my career path has differed from Daddy's. I get paid to do something I love and I'm lucky enough that it means I can provide for my family. It's not an easy vocation but it's a great one.

I've never had to worry about doing a job I wasn't completely invested in. Maybe that day will come in my post-footy career, but I must admit the idea feels alien to me. Sure, at times I wasn't all that enamoured with football but, for the most part, it's been a pretty amazing job.

Both my parents did what they had to do to make sure we had everything we needed. When you're young, you don't really pay any attention to these things. You just know that food and footy gear just kind of appear when you need them, that's how things work.

While Daddy's chosen career provided stability, it wasn't an easy occupation for him, or for Mammy. In the early days before Mammy and Daddy moved to Summerhill Lane, our house was close enough to the prison to hear 'the alarm' go off. This was before mobile phones were so ubiquitous. Daddy wouldn't get a call saying he needed to go into work urgently to search an inmate's cell or deal with a security issue, he would simply hear the alarm and immediately spring into action, even if he wasn't rostered on that day. I don't remember the alarm, and I didn't have any awareness of what he did for a living. I just remember his uniform.

Every day, he would put on the same pale-blue shirt and head off to work. When I think of my father during my childhood, I just see him in that shirt. The same way a superhero always has the same outfit on, that's how I think of him – like 'Prison-man'. He also had a hat, a baton and a silver whistle. I didn't know what the baton was for, but that didn't stop me playing with it while wearing his hat and swinging his silver trench whistle by its chain. I thought I cut quite the imposing figure striding around the house enforcing my own martial law.

As far as I was concerned, Daddy's job wasn't unusual and it never occurred to me that it was dangerous, it was just what he did. He could have been a postman for all I knew. The reality is, and it's something I only appreciate now, he worked in a maximum-security prison that housed some of the country's most notorious criminals, as well as those incarcerated for paramilitary activity and membership of the IRA (Irish Republican Army). As an adult, with two kids of my own, I marvel at my parents' ability to shield me from what he did to put food on the table, especially during times of turbulence in the prison.

Daddy's occupation meant he mixed with some colourful, high-profile and, in some cases, infamous characters. He made the most of the opportunity to interact and learn from these people. He would have regular debates with prisoners in the library. Locking horns with them over everything from politics to life. Those debates ended up being a precursor to his career in politics. Passionate debates on topics he truly cared about, listening to opposing views and then countering them in his charming and witty way. Daddy has the ability to disarm and dismantle your point of view and still ensure you leave the room with a smile on your face. He didn't need to raise his baton at work, the spoken word was his weapon of choice.

In a workplace that is by its very nature dark and sombre, his witty exchanges uplifted everyone, including the prisoners. When I ask Daddy about his memories of working there, he'll always recount the lighter moments first.

'E1 landing' (an area in the E-Block of the prison) is where a lot of the heavy hitters were housed, including Ireland's most infamous gangster John Gilligan, convicted drug dealer Christy Kinahan, and garda killers Colm O'Shea and Paddy McCann. Then there was convicted armed robber John Daly, who famously called one of Ireland's most popular radio shows – *Liveline* with Joe Duffy – from his prison cell, on a phone that was smuggled in. The prison officers heard the interview live and confiscated the phone and SIM card immediately, a story that always makes me chuckle when Daddy tells it. Because of this incident, there was a significant crackdown on contraband in the prison, which Daly's fellow prisoners did not appreciate.

The problem for prison officers isn't just the risk of being attacked themselves, but also of getting seriously injured while trying to break up fights between prisoners.

Daddy remembers an incident involving his good friend John 'Ulick' Conroy, who was in charge of the E1 block. The prisoners were going off again, all hell had broken loose. There's only so much officers can do in that situation, especially when they're outnumbered. They did what they could while preserving their safety as best they could and, eventually, the place calmed down. Ulick was then raked over the coals by the chief officer and asked why he hadn't stepped in and taken control immediately – as though these were kindergarten kids they were talking about. My dad fondly remembers Ulick's response: 'Well, chief, you see my name is John Conroy, not John Wayne.'

The prison alarm meant something different to Mammy than it did Daddy. For Daddy, it was simply a yell from the boss: 'Your shift starts now, Noel!' But for Mammy it meant that something unexpected had happened and somebody needed to go fix it. And when something unexpected happens in a maximum-security prison, she could be forgiven for being concerned that her husband was the one who had to go and take care of it.

However, when pushing Mammy for more details about some of these 'alarm stories', as we call them, one stands out.

One morning, breakfast was again interrupted by the

shriek of the prison alarm, and off Daddy went. Another 7 a.m. search of a prisoner's cell.

His home time came and went, and there was no sign of Daddy.

FUCK! my mother thought. *What's happened?*

Back then, when you called the prison, they wouldn't tell you anything. Good or bad, they would always keep their cards close to their chest. I don't know if this was protocol or just the way things worked, but the result was always the same for Mammy – no answers and no reassurances.

Later in the evening, there was a knock on the front door.

It was a neighbour whose husband also worked at the prison. Mammy had never met her before.

'Is your husband missing too?' she asked.

'Yeah,' Mammy replied.

The neighbour was brandishing a bottle of brandy in one hand and a bottle of vodka in the other.

After a glass of brandy and a chat, Mammy says she thought she knew where the duo might be and, not long after, her suspicions were confirmed.

Daddy had gone into work at 7 a.m., had an uneventful morning and finished by 10 a.m. A work colleague of his, Arthur Costello, ran a pub called The Thatch and had graciously offered to open it for them.

No man in his right mind could turn down such a

generous offer, so off they went – a group of about 10. And after a fun-filled day, Daddy returned home.

Guinness had been the drink of choice, and it was a fine pint too, as Daddy proclaimed as he walked through the front door.

However, Mammy, now half a bottle of brandy in, wasn't as eager to hear Daddy's tasting notes as he'd hoped and demanded to know why he'd chosen radio silence over a phone call. But as this was still the best-case scenario, Mammy quickly got over her anger and turned to relief. Laughter, jokes and a few more drinks were the order for the remainder of the evening. All was well.

Daddy had brought company – his fellow prison officer Noel Burke was with him. Noel had come seeking refuge and a place to sober up before heading home himself. This was a humanitarian issue of the utmost importance. It would have been unjust to send a man home to face the wrath of an understandably angry wife (she also had no idea if he was okay) without at least providing him the opportunity to sober up and ready himself for battle. Mammy and Daddy of course obliged, and Mammy began to cook up whatever she could find in the fridge.

Armed with a full belly and newfound courage, Noel Burke calmly strode out the front door and headed straight back to the pub. What a man.

Growing up, my siblings and I were oblivious to the dangers of Daddy's job. Mammy made sure of that.

At one point, there was what could have been an empty threat, but a threat nonetheless, made against prison officers that they would be targeted by car bombs. Which, to be fair, would be very much on brand for some of the inhabitants of Portlaoise prison. It was not the type of thing you ignored, so prison officers were told they should check under their cars every morning in case anything suspicious had been placed there. Our neighbours saw the story in the news and when Daddy was asked if he was worried about it, he always said the same thing.

'Not worried at all. Marie usually goes out and starts the car in the morning,' he'd laugh.

Daddy always used humour as a shield. It was his way of playing down the risk of what he did.

As I write this, it occurs to me that that is exactly what I've done my whole life. It's almost as if we're related.

Despite what you've read so far, you might be surprised to hear that it's actually my mother who is the tough one in the family. The one you'd send to fight your battles, if necessary. Stern in her convictions and ferociously protective of her kids is how I'd describe her.

I mean, sure, Daddy was a prison officer. But I would much prefer to take him on than her. All of the women in our family are strong. First to jump from the trenches into battle when family honour is on the line. Don't get me wrong – most of the time they are gentle and kind. But I have become convinced that they are, in fact, part-gremlin as they seem to share their ability to transform into aggressive little monsters, but only when called for.

Now that I've written that, I think I might be bad at analogies because that was meant to be a compliment. I'm not sure calling your mother and sisters monsters constitutes flattery.

Nonethelesss, my inability to adequately articulate, in a complimentary way, just how tough the women in my family are doesn't change the fact that they are tough. As I get older, I can't help but notice that my two older sisters – Naomi and Hannah – are evolving into the same type of matriarch as Mammy.

Even now, if I had to pick someone to go into a meeting because my job was on the line, I'd pick my mother. When we were growing up, Mammy was always the disciplinarian, while Daddy was the supplier of endless ice creams and treats. Because Daddy never said no, that became her job, and she gladly took it on.

She would also happily take on anyone who dared to cross her family. I remember one incident when I was playing football in secondary school, what Australians would call 'high school'. We had a game in the morning, then PE in the afternoon and, after all of that, I was scheduled to play an Under-14 county final in the evening.

Mammy called the school to say she was going to keep

me out of PE class, which made sense. But the principal of the school – who embodied the typical Christian Brothers-style of education, shall we call it – didn't like it. He called the house phone and when my sister Naomi answered he said, 'We're going to suspend Zach for a few days because he didn't come back to school after lunch.'

The following week, he called again and asked where I was, as I was required for an inter-school football match. Even though I was suspended, they needed their best players.

'Mammy has decided to send Zach to a new school,' my sister Naomi announced.

The principal quickly backtracked on everything he had said just days earlier and we never had an issue with him again. From that moment on, my mother managed my PE and training schedule without complaint from him. She would never have taken me out of that school, but she was happy to make that threat. This was standard Mammy practice.

Mammy's unwavering support for my career falls just short of actually watching the games. Her usual vantage point for any county final or major game I've been involved in is at the back of the stand or pacing around the garden. If she does have the field in her eyeline, her standard pose is the good old reliable head in hands, unable to watch, as her nerves get the better of her.

I honestly thought this was just a Mammy thing until early 2019 when I spent my first major stint on the sidelines and realised I'm exactly the same. When forced to watch my team play without me, I was desperate to leave my seat and retreat to the safety of the pie stand. But that wouldn't have been a great look. I'm turning into Mammy. Every young bloke's dream.

The best example of my mother missing out on a big moment in my career because she couldn't handle the crushing suspense of a tight match came late in the 2018 season when we took on Melbourne on a cold and windy Friday night at GMHBA stadium. (GMHBA is a health insurance company that sponsors Geelong's home stadium, locally it's also known as Kardinia Park. For us it's just a fortress – a place we rarely lose.) We were down by 29 at three-quarter-time and a hero was needed. A big ol' sexy Irish hero, I might add.

But I'll finish that story later.

As I said, my old man was always the one to cave under pressure from my siblings and I when we were asking for a toy or ice cream or whatever was tickling our fancy at that moment. I'm sure the armchair psychiatrists out there might come to the conclusion that because my father had to impose strict rules at work, he didn't want to do the same at home for fear of making it feel like a mini prison to him, or making his own children feel like mini inmates. Very clever and perceptive of you – but it's not true.

In the prison, all the officers had nicknames. One of them was called 'Ten to Two' because his feet were always spread a certain way – they thought he stood like a penguin. Then there was 'Digger', 'Saddle Head' and 'Half Door'. My old man's nickname was 'The Nice Guy'. In his entire career, he never took out that baton I played with – not once.

My old man never felt it was his job to impose rules on anybody at work. In his view, his job wasn't to punish the prisoners – the state had already done that. It was his job to facilitate their life. He was very aware that his work conditions were their life conditions. He treated them with respect. And he has always been cause-driven – always wanting to stick up for the little guy. These characteristics are another reason his subsequent career in politics as a county councillor was hardly surprising. He served as a councillor in Portlaoise from 2014 to 2022, when he retired.

So, my dad wasn't 'the endless supplier of treats' at home because of his work; he just couldn't say no to his kids. Noel Tuohy: 'The Nice Guy' nickname applied at home too.

Away from work, he was the life of the party and at the heart of the community. Every year, he starred in the local pantomime, and I loved going to watch him. They performed a different production every year but there's one year in particular I remember vividly. This performance featured pirates. Said pirates would run off the stage and grab some of the kids in the crowd to bring them on stage. I would always get picked out of the crowd or mentioned during the performance. As a 10-year-old, this was very cool. Daddy still performed in the panto until a few years ago.

Despite working long hours and unsociable shifts, Daddy always made sure he was there for us. He came home every day for lunch so he could see us. We weren't allowed to go to bed until he was home, which was almost nine o'clock some nights. He never, ever, missed a football match I played in, regardless of where in the country it was. Even if he worked all night, he would drive for hours to see me play. I remember we played the Kennedy Cup in Limerick – a soccer tournament played over five days, and let's just say the standard wasn't great. I don't know how he managed it, but he and Mammy made the three-hour round trip daily, to watch all of my matches.

Daddy always says that as a parent your goal in life has to be to give your kids a better life than you had, whatever that might be. Now as an adult, I find that impossible because, as far as I'm concerned, I couldn't have had it any better growing up.

It wasn't just my parents who made sure I had everything I needed. My grandmother, Hannah, on my dad's side, lived close to us. She had 11 grandchildren, but it was a well-known fact in the Tuohy clan that I was the undisputed favourite. This was not something that she tried to hide; in fact, she made it very obvious to my cousins (sorry, cousins!).

In Ireland, it's common for Catholics to light a candle for someone in church when they want to say a special prayer for them. My grandmother didn't need to go to church to light a candle for me, she had her own set up at home. She literally built a shrine to me in the house. When you walked in, there was an area with framed photos of me surrounded by candles. If you went to visit and you didn't know any better, you'd think I was dead.

Granny's house was the tenth in a row of terraced houses in Marian Avenue – the very same house my father had grown up in. Each one had a small and identical front garden, but Granny's house was unmistakably hers. If Granny wasn't sitting on the waist-high wall that wrapped around her little garden, waiting for someone to stop by, she would be sitting in her armchair in the living room, which was placed right next to the window looking out onto the street. It was almost as if she was on guard, protecting the house from any would-be intruders, like an elderly German shepherd.

As you entered Granny's house, a short hallway guided you towards the living room where there would almost always be a fire lit, and two or three visitors on the couch watching an old western show on the TV.

The Virginian was usually the show of choice.

She was unashamed in her favouritism, which is funny to look back at now, but she was always more interested in spending time with me over anyone else.

One of my earliest memories of her is how she would let me watch TV in her room, while she delivered rice bubbles with hot milk. And then there were Hot Lips Tayto crisps, my other favourite snack. There was an unlimited supply of those for me at Granny's. For Australians who may not be familiar with Tayto crisps, just know that they are as important to our Irish palate as Vegemite is to Australians. While classic 'Cheese and Onion' is everyone's favourite, I preferred the less conventional 'Hot Lips'. You could say I had a more adventurous approach to snacks from an early age, or you could just say I was spoiled rotten.

Hot Lips were my catnip – I couldn't help myself – and a drawer full of them in Granny's kitchen meant I would never go without.

She also supplied me with endless pocket money. If I needed it, I would just pop over to her house. She'd give me whatever cash she had handy at the time, sometimes 20 or 30 pounds (big money back then). This meant I was able to buy as many English Premier League collector cards as I wanted.

I remember, one time, Naomi bought Granny one of those picture frames you could open out and put multiple photos into. There were about 10 spaces for pictures and Naomi had thoughtfully filled them up with snapshots of all the grandkids. On receipt of the present, my granny removed all the photos and replaced them with photos of me – only me. We still laugh about that when I'm back home.

When I moved to Australia, Granny gave me a little pocket watch that had been blessed in Lourdes. It is bound to a small red leather case by a short chain. It hasn't accurately told the time in years, but that has never really been its purpose for me – it's what it represents. It was Granny's attempt to try to protect me in some way, when I was on the other side of the world. I'm not religious, but I still keep it in my car and, to this day, it hangs from my rear-view mirror. For those who are curious about my tattoos, its image is also permanently etched onto the back of my forearm, such is its sentimental value to me. It is one of my most treasured possessions.

The Premier League cards she helped me fund were just the start of what's been a lifelong passion for soccer and, more specifically, for Liverpool Football Club. A huge highlight growing up was when Daddy took me to Anfield to see them play when I was 12 years old. I love that he took us on adventures like that at such a young age, instead of waiting until we were older.

But then, Daddy never made us wait to experience the joy of sport. He turned up at my school one day to surprise me with a new set of golf clubs. He knocked on the classroom door at 11 a.m. before promptly taking me out for the rest of the day so we could go to the local par-three golf course to try them out.

My mother would let us have the odd day off school. We were allowed to have one day off, per term, of our choosing. Any day we wanted. This was obviously a major decision and Mammy says I would often decide that I was going to take a day off and then she would see me coming down the stairs in my uniform, because I had reconsidered my selection and wanted to save it for a really, really good day – like if I had a test or something. I remember trying to get a Friday off one time because I hadn't done my homework the night before (a regular occurrence). In a lot of Irish secondary schools, including ours, Fridays were half-days and I remember Mammy saying very seriously, 'Why would you do that?' She was as concerned as I was that I use my day off wisely.

Going to see Liverpool play for the first time is still one of my all-time favourite sporting memories. Dad and I got the ferry over to England – and that could be a gruelling experience. Sometimes, that crossing was so choppy it was like an episode of *Deadliest Catch*. There was one trip where everyone was so ill that when I went into the bathroom all the sinks were filled with vomit. On that fateful trip, we were sitting next to a group of young lads on a stag do. They were doing okay, but one of them was struggling. His friends gave him a vomit bag, but they'd cut the bottom out of it as a prank, so he was sick all over himself. They erupted with laughter as I watched on. The poor bastard. I don't remember if I ever got sick on our trips, I just remember that every time we went to watch Liverpool, they won.

On that first trip to Anfield, Liverpool defeated Bayer Leverkusen 1–0 in the Champions League. Sami Hyypiä scored the winner. But it was what happened the day after that made the trip epic. My dad loved horse racing, so we went to Aintree and there was this one race with a massive field, about 30 horses. Daddy asked me to pick a winner, and I did – based off the colours I liked. I picked Torduff

Express, and Daddy was offered great odds, about 10/1. He put £15 on it, and we settled in to watch.

I'll never forget the feeling of watching Torduff Express take the lead after clearing the last ditch. Back then, my racing attire wasn't up to Melbourne Cup standard. In my view, it was better. I was proudly wearing my Liverpool jersey, as Daddy and I cheered Torduff Express home. He won by 10 or 12 lengths, and we were ecstatic. When Daddy came back from collecting his winnings, he gave me £15. To me, this was massive. I didn't realise how much he was pocketing for himself, which he often reminds me of. If there had been merchandise for Torduff Express, I would have bought it with my winnings. To add to the Liverpool tour kit.

I look back on that trip and think about how lucky I was. Even for an adult sports tragic, that trip is bucket-list standard. I was living my best life at 12.

Because the English Premier League and Liverpool, coupled with dreams of playing soccer professionally, consumed my thoughts, you might be surprised to hear that I had very little interest in watching my county team – Laois – play Gaelic football at the time. It's not that I didn't love playing Gaelic football, but if I was sitting down to watch sport for the day, English Premier League games were what I automatically gravitated towards. I could watch endless hours of soccer. It was the first professional sport I watched, and I just wanted to be one of them. I thought that was my only chance of playing football professionally.

Despite my lack of enthusiasm at the time, my dad would take us kids to all of Laois' matches in Croke Park. It was really cool but, back then, I only had thoughts of Liverpool.

I remember when the FA Cup trophy visited Portlaoise and we all went for photos. The trophy was touring after Liverpool won it in 2001. It was probably an imitation trophy but, to me, it was the real deal, and having a photo with it was a massive thrill.

My dad wasn't the only one who treated me to weekends away. My older brother, Noel John, is responsible for one of my most memorable early-teenage experiences. He brought me to my first concert. He's a heavy metal kind of guy, and his concert of choice was Metallica. I was 14 at the time and he was 20. I went up to Dublin to stay with him in his tiny apartment. He bought me a few cans of beer and off we went. I was pissed after two cans, and I loved the gig. His influence on my musical taste has endured to this day, and even played a part in my Grand Final experience.

It was my first big night out in the big smoke. When we went back to the apartment, all of my brother's friends were smoking weed. I really wanted to try it, but my brother wouldn't let me because he's clearly a very responsible adult – quite happy to feed alcohol to a 14-year-old, but weed? Never.

Despite his best intentions, it was a small, not very well-ventilated apartment, so while he stopped me from having my own joint, it's fair to say that I consumed it anyway. I was hotboxing. I'd never done this before so wasn't aware of the effect it was having on me. Neither was my brother. Fast forward a few hours, and Noel John noticed I'd been in the toilet for a while, so he went to check on me. And what he found was, as he describes it, a Frankenstein monster of his own creation. I was stood in the bathroom laughing hysterically at the German toothpaste that belonged to my brother's then girlfriend, who was Austrian. It was then that the realisation hit him that what was meant to be a lovely brotherly night out had turned into some Irish version of a *Cheech & Chong* skit.

Noel John spent the next hour warning me that if Mammy called, I had to straighten myself up. Unfortunately for him, his pleas fell on deaf ears and instead of straightening up, I found it much more entertaining to repeat everything he said to me, using my best Noel John impersonation. Luckily for him, Mammy didn't call.

It turned out to be my penultimate attempt at taking drugs. On one other occasion when I was in university, my friends and I decided we would try smoking. Noel John had kindly bought some hash and even gave us a demonstration on how to roll it, only to receive a call 15 minutes later asking him to come back, because we were making an awful balls of our subsequent construction attempts. We just couldn't figure out how to do it. And that, believe it or not, was it. I retired from recreational drug use and didn't look back. The extent of my drug dabbling can be summed up quickly, in two underwhelming experiences.

Maybe these rather harmless and unsuccessful ventures into recreational drug-taking were what turned me off for good, and I never felt tempted to re-enter that space as an adult.

When I look back at those times, it's not lost on me how lucky I was and am. Living on the other side of the world isn't easy, especially when you're from a tight-knit family. But any success that I experience in Australia, I wear as a badge of honour for my family, because they gave me the perfect start in life.

My parents taught me to work hard and stick with it, even when times are tough, to persevere and push through in pursuit of your goal. When there have been times that I didn't think I could go on, I got through it because they had instilled that lesson in me.

'The child is father of the man' is one of my favourite quotations. It's from a William Wordsworth poem 'My Heart Leaps Up', which was published in 1807.

While I always appreciated the meaning of that quotation – that how you are shaped as a child will have a big effect on who you grow up to be as an adult – and the amazing foundation my parents provided for me as a child, it would only truly hit home when my first son, Flynn, was born years later.

CHAPTER 2

The Confidence Trick

NOW, I KNOW YOU LOOK AT ME TODAY AND think, *Jesus, the women must love Zach because he's so funny and sexy and he's probably great in bed,* and that's all true, especially the last one. But it hasn't always been the case. In fact, quite the opposite.

In my early teens, I would approach women the same way the bomb squad approaches an unattended suitcase in an airport – with extreme caution, knowing that the best-case scenario was that I'd get out of there uninjured and the worst-case scenario was that the whole thing would blow up in my face.

On the rare occasion when my interest was reciprocated, I'd think there was something wrong with her because ... I mean ... seriously?

Me? That's the best you can do?

It was around this time that Gaelic football was really beginning to ramp up in my life and I was starting to take it very seriously. When it came to the sport I consumed on TV, however, my priority was still the English Premier League, but I had started to accept that I was more skilled in GAA than soccer.

At underage level, I was constantly anxious about how I would perform in GAA games. Because our club and school were so successful, a high standard was always expected, and I felt the pressure of that. In soccer, a sport in which I ended up representing the Midlands team, I felt no expectation to perform, so I played more freely and I didn't doubt myself as much. But Gaelic football was the main sport in our school, so it naturally consumed a lot of my time.

While I felt I wasn't good at it, there was a lot of evidence to the contrary. I was actually decent – I even excelled at it – but I lacked confidence.

If I lacked confidence with something I was genuinely good at, can you even imagine how little belief I brought to my pursuit of women? I thought I was useless in this area but, when I look back on it, I was probably as competent as most young lads of my age.

It certainly didn't feel that way, though.

I have the quirky personality trait of being reasonably extroverted around people I'm close to and extremely introverted around everyone else. Fourteen-year-old me really struggled to chat to new people, never mind girls. I mean, what would I say to them?

My attempted conversations were usually uncomfortable and tense, with neither party benefiting from the exchange nor wanting to be there in general. It more closely resembled a hostage negotiation than a teenage flirtation.

I think I was probably regarded as fun-loving and extroverted by my school friends and teammates, so their assumption was that this would carry over into other parts of my life ... I wish.

My father, on the other hand, is a socialite – the life and soul of the party. The men in our family all share the same preoccupation with humour. It's only as an adult that I've realised, in my case at least, that this is what I used to compensate for my innate shyness.

It's been said that I'm quite witty, but when it comes to comedic ability, I barely crack the top three in the Tuohy house. My older brother, Noel John, is genuinely gifted when it comes to comedy. He is highly creative and I've no doubt he would be capable of a successful career as a stand-up comedian if he decided to pursue that. There is no better example of this than when he gave his best-man speech at my wedding. The uncontrollable laughter he inspired highlighted even further just how far behind I am in the chase for the title of 'funniest Tuohy'.

So, I come from funny stock and have combined that with years of practice at using my humour to offset my timid nature. Because of that, I've never been short of male friends, but, unfortunately, have not been so successful with the fairer sex. Mainly because when a girl I was interested in entered the conversation, I would instantly go mute. They would not be the beneficiary of my comedic material. Oh no – I would just look at them awkwardly.

What made my self-doubt worse was, because I was a good footballer, I tended to move in 'cool' circles. When you play Gaelic football growing up, you represent your local area. For me, that was Portlaoise. If you were talented enough, you were given the opportunity to play a couple of age groups up, because they considered you ready and, if you were really lucky, you got to represent your county. I was starting to show signs I could do that, which meant I was fraternising with older players or county players who I'd met at training. (By the way, when I say I was showing signs, I should point out that I didn't think I was anything special – quite the opposite in fact – but more on that later.)

As far as I was concerned, I was deeply uncool, so I would watch as my mates effortlessly chatted to girls they liked. *Incredible*, I thought. *How could anyone ever be so courageous as to actually walk up to a woman and speak to her?* Jesus, in my view, that level of courage was reserved for deep-sea explorers.

By the time our friendship group turned 15, we started having a few drinks before heading out. Nothing crazy, just enough to get us on our way. Yes, the legal limit for drinking in Ireland is 18, just like Australia, but, if we were going out, we always managed to find a way of getting our hands on a few cans. Usually, we would ask one of the older footballers at the club to go and buy some for us. It would, of course, only take two or three drinks for us to be 'happy', shall we call it. More often than not, we would drink at someone's house if their parents were away but, on the odd occasion we couldn't find a free house, we would pick somewhere quiet and secluded outdoors to enjoy our beverages. Even if it was freezing, we remained undeterred. Alfresco drinking was a big part of our social schedule, regardless of the weather.

Sitting together in a park or a field away from prying eyes, we would drink our two or three cans and head off to whatever disco or club would let us in. Hardly the classiest evening, but this is the kind of environment my friends and I thrived in. There's no doubt that my most enduring friendships were forged over a cold beer and singsong.

Another spot we would occasionally begin our nights out at was the snooker hall – yet another sport I became infatuated with for a period. How much it cost to play depended on how long the frame went on for. The light above the table was turned on the start of a frame and would defectively act as a stopwatch. The longer the frame took – i.e. the longer the light was on – the more the frame would cost. Because of the payment situation, the most common wager in the snooker hall was to 'play for lights', with the loser footing the bill. Losing was expensive and this helped my skills.

My love of snooker and pool was cultivated further by my parents who, one Christmas, bought us – but to be honest, mostly bought me – a pool table. They bought the table from a pub in Tipperary six weeks before Christmas and put it in the garage. Pool tables are pretty conspicuous, so they had a hard time ensuring I didn't wander in there during that time. I was over the moon when Christmas morning arrived. Of all the gifts they've given me over the years, and there have been many, this was the best.

The Christmas present meant that our garage was effectively converted into my pool room. I would have mates around to play and listen to music and all was well in the world. No more 'alfresco' drinking for me; we were living it up at Château Tuohy.

These kinds of shenanigans are important. I really believe that. At that age, teenagers just need to be around their friends – to feel like they're not alone and have a safe space to be idiots. And idiots we were. I truly believe that, in a way, we are kids at heart our whole lives, and sports clubs provide a chance to let loose and have fun. There was nothing deep or meaningful about our change room. Yes, we were all working towards a common goal, but at the end of the day, we were just having fun most of the time.

Mind you, there were long periods where our shenanigans were curtailed and there was no drinking at all, 'alfresco' or not. Despite being an amateur sport, drinking bans are common in Gaelic football. So, yes, even in club ranks, when you have a big game coming up, you can be banned from consuming any alcohol at all. I can safely say I've had more opportunities to go on nights out as a professional footballer than I did when I was playing amateur football. In GAA, your club and/or county can ask you to go completely cold turkey for months. I mean, it was probably for the best. We could have caught frostbite on some of those outdoor sessions.

Fitting in, at that age, was just about the most important thing in the world to me. Nights like that meant a lot because I didn't always feel like I did. My insecurities weren't restricted to girls; in my early teens I worried about not being liked and being ostracised from my friendship group. I think all kids worry about that.

I remember one crushing blow in the friendship ranks, when I was about 14. I grew up at the back of our housing estate, on a long lane with friends occupying houses at either end of the street and my family home in the middle. We were perfectly placed for the boys to call past and collect me for footballing exploits or to get up to no good.

One Saturday afternoon, I happened to be upstairs looking out the window onto the lane and spotted some friends walking towards my house with football in hand. I started getting my football gear on in readiness to answer the door ... but there was no knock on the door. When I looked out the window to check on the delay, I watched as they all carried on up the lane without me. Which was fine, I thought, they were clearly just heading up the road to recruit extra players and would loop back to get me on the way back.

Instead, I watched them all continue out of the lane and up the hill towards the park we played soccer in. They'd never intended on asking me to come and join them. I was gutted.

I know this doesn't seem like a big deal but, back then, it was huge. And that wasn't even the worst part.

Not long after, there was a knock on our front door; it was the lads. *How bloody good*, I thought. *They must have just forgotten to come and get me or thought I wasn't home but figured they should come back and check just to be sure.* Delighted and relieved, I began to walk out and towards the park where we always played.

'It's too wet,' they said. 'We were wondering if we could use your tennis court instead.'

Our house had a tennis court out the back, which had been turned into a small pitch with goals at either end. It was tarmac and therefore not rain-logged like the football pitch. These pricks didn't want me to come play with them at all, they just wanted to use my facilities because it had started to rain. What I should have done was told them to go and get fucked and slammed the door in their faces, but that would have required far more confidence than I could muster at the time, so instead I just went along with it and invited them all in. These were, and are, some of my best friends to this day, but that seemingly insignificant slight hurt for a long time.

A sidenote about this tennis court. I know what you're thinking: *He had a tennis court as well as a pool room?* My mother often says Daddy prioritised my sporting endeavours over my education, and perhaps she's right. Thankfully, it worked out pretty well in the end. The tennis court was put in when I was very young but was soon converted into a soccer pitch after we removed the net and placed goals at either end. The goals were, of course, another Christmas present from my parents. I'm starting to see a trend here.

The original tennis court was laid out the back after our parents gave us a generous ultimatum. They told us we could either go on a holiday or get a tennis court. It went to a siblings' vote. I was only four or five years old at the time, so I'm not sure my vote counted, but I know I would have put my hand up for tennis, of course. Thankfully, Hannah, Naomi and Noel John were of the same mind. That tennis court provided countless hours of fun and was the perfect home-training facility for an aspiring athlete.

As the years progressed, it was mainly me using the tennis court as my siblings became less and less interested in sport. However, I didn't often use it for tennis. The net could be taken down and stored in the shed when a game of basketball broke out or my friends were around to play football. Unfortunately, the basketball games didn't last long because of the weather. The net, which was held up by a deeply rooted steel pole, was upended in a storm and never repaired – so the tennis court gradually morphed into an almost exclusively football-focused facility.

Back to our successful pool nights at chez Zach. Sometimes after a few games, we'd board the bus in Portlaoise and head to the neighbouring town of Tullamore, to the infamous Harriers, which was a teenage disco. I can see all my mates giggling at the mere mention of the Harriers as they read this.

While it only takes Tullamore Dew 12 to 15 years to mature, it would, as it turns out, take me a lot longer.

You had to be 16 to get into Harriers and they checked your ID at the door. Standard practice was to borrow someone else's ID and hope the resemblance was strong enough and the bouncer was sufficiently distracted or, even better, too uninterested to check properly – and then bang, in you went.

Spoiler alert – I almost never got in.

That didn't stop me trying, though.

The main issue with not getting in was that you had to

wait until the end of the night for the bus to come back, so you were left just standing outside. Fortunately – or unfortunately, depending on your perspective – there were usually as many people outside as there were inside. So, you certainly weren't alone, but this did mean that there were a lot of angry drunk teens mingling together. You were only ever one smart comment away from a fight breaking out.

On one occasion a friend and I didn't get in and were keeping our distance to try to avoid trouble, only for the gardaí (police for my Australian friends) to pull up and start questioning us. We hadn't done anything wrong, but for absolutely no reason I decided to lie about my name and where I was from. Again, no need whatsoever to do this but, sure, why not risk getting arrested to really cap off a great night? When I offered my convincing fake name, I could see the panic on my friend's face. He was not expecting this, but he followed suit and plucked from nowhere a completely made-up name like Harry Jones or something.

Luckily, they accepted what we said. I mean, you'd have to be a complete idiot to lie in that situation for absolutely no reason, right?

Clearly undeterred by the garda presence in the town, we thought we'd have a crack at saving the night. Off we went to a random pub in Tullamore town in the hope of being served a nice, creamy pint. Just because we couldn't convince the Harriers bouncers we were 16 didn't mean we couldn't convince the barman we were 18 …

Now, I know you're all expecting me to say we obviously didn't get served and that we had to leave the pub with our tails between our legs. And, yes, you're right.

Back to Harriers we went, to wait for the bus back to Portlaoise, from the disco we never went to. There you have it – a glimpse into the glamour of my teens.

Despite the setbacks, these were some of the best nights out of my adolescence.

I was pretty good at dealing with rejection from bouncers, but I found rejection in other areas of my life tough. Every time I added a rejection to the pile, I took it as confirmation that I was mediocre. A mediocre footballer, a mediocre bloke or mediocre with girls.

My negative self-perception and self-talk just kept doing its best to convince me I was what I feared most: mediocre. I didn't want to be mediocre; I wanted to be a high-end performer in every way.

I figured the best way to avoid rejection was to avoid being in situations where rejection was a possible outcome. This meant I never tried out for the intercounty team. And when I was asked to join our school's senior team as a 14-year-old, I declined (more on this later). And, my God, you couldn't pay me enough money to peacock my way over to a girl to chat her up, as that level of rejection would have been too much to handle.

Looking back, I don't really know why I struggled with confidence so much. Things were, for the most part, really good. If I could go back and give one piece of advice to my younger self, it would be just that – you're doing fine, mate. I would reassure myself that I wasn't the only bloke going through this, and the perception I had of myself didn't match the world's perception of me at all. I would tell myself that uncomfortable situations aren't something to be feared or avoided, but rather to be sought out and used as a catalyst for growth and improvement. That it's not smart to avoid these situations – you're depriving yourself of opportunities to improve. I wish someone could have told me that. I think the younger me would have appreciated it.

I know some people look back fondly on their teens, even longing to go back and relive them. Not for me. Yes, there were a lot of great times but I couldn't be happier that those days are behind me.

Now, I mentioned briefly that I turned down the opportunity to be part of my school's senior football team. This was a strange one. It came at a time when I was beginning to show what I was capable of as a footballer. I still didn't feel like one of the better players in my age bracket, but clearly other people viewed me that way. It was yet another example of my perception of myself not matching everyone else's perception of me. I was one of only two Second Year students (that's Year 9 for Australian readers) who were invited to join the senior team.

Around this time, Laois underage football was incredibly strong; they'd won multiple minor provincial titles and achieved All-Ireland minor success in 2003. A lot of these players were in my school, so our senior team was loaded with talent. Although I was invited to join, I didn't think I was good enough.

It wasn't just that I didn't think I deserved to be there, I was also too shy to be there. I was 14, and most of the players in the squad were 16 or 17 years old. As mentioned, some of these guys had already won a minor All-Ireland title. I went to a couple of training sessions, but shyness got the better of me and I pulled myself off the team.

This team would go on to narrowly lose the All-Ireland Colleges senior football championship (SFC) 'B' final. What an experience that would have been. I look back on it as one of my greatest missed opportunities, but, paradoxically, it was an important mistake to make. I learned a valuable lesson. I was never going to miss an opportunity like that again. At some point, I had to stop letting myself get in the way of my own career.

I often use this as an important point of reference. Not just in sport, but in life too.

From then on, if my hard work or natural talent opened doors for me, I wasn't going to let my timid – what I perceived to be 'cowardly' – nature close them. Not anymore, those days were gone. From then on, even if a door was just ajar, I would charge through and, if it didn't work out, then so be it. I'd prefer that to the 'what ifs'.

I now had a new attitude, a 'yes' approach, but, despite the fact I was being selected for teams years ahead of my peer group, I still lacked belief in my ability. To everyone else, from my coaches to my teammates, it was obvious, but I just wasn't there yet.

It wasn't until I was turning 16 that I realised I had the potential to excel past my peers.

Today, friends and former coaches will say they could tell early on that I was extremely talented. That they knew I would go on to achieve great things. I'm not sure if they are just rewriting history or if they did see something in me that I couldn't.

As well as my school team being stacked with talent, Portlaoise GAA boasted the most talented crop of players in the club's history at the time. Kieran Lillis, Paul Cahillane, Brian Glynn, Brian Smith and Conor Boyle would all go on to play senior intercounty football and make up the nucleus of a Portlaoise team that would dominate club football in our county for 15 years.

Our group won every championship at every age group, from Under-12s right through to seniors. Standards were high and competition for spots was intense.

I grew up playing corner-back and would eventually graduate to centre-back as I developed, but that was likely to be as far forward as I would move, positionally. I didn't think I could play midfield because I wasn't dominant enough in the air. Although I was technically skilful enough to play in the front half, I probably didn't have the composure at that point. So, centre-back it was, and, at that time, it suited me perfectly, as I had the physical attributes to excel there. Basically, I was strong and fast. I was a reliable, six-or-seven-out-of-ten-every-week type of player ... and then there was Paul.

Paul Cahillane, a great friend of mine to this day, was so exceptionally talented at the time, it was almost unfair. He would run rings around everyone in both football and soccer, and was clearly far too good to be playing at local level. It didn't take long for him to garner the attention of scouts from different clubs in Ireland and the UK. At 16 years of age, he was signed by Celtic Football Club. Incredible. One of our mates was a professional athlete. *This is dream stuff*, I thought. I could hardly believe it. I was extremely proud of him, of course, but also envious that he had done it. I was 15 at the time and, despite my exploits in the Kennedy Cup (a soccer competition), the scouts were not calling me.

Despite my love of soccer, I never attracted interest. As far as I was concerned, when Paul headed off, and I was still in Portlaoise, the ship that was professional sport seemed like it had well and truly sailed.

Despite the fact I'd never play soccer professionally, I loved playing with my friends. One evening, while playing on an astroturf pitch, someone stood on my foot. Being stood on wasn't at all unusual, but the intense and immediate pain in the aftermath that time was. I couldn't walk or put any pressure on it at all. I went home and did what I always did – I assumed it would be fine. I iced it and went to bed. The next morning, my foot was twice its normal size and resembled one big bruise. It was ugly – and painful.

Off I went for an x-ray and, sure enough, it required surgery. At the time, the surgeon told Mammy it was actually an old break. He had to put a pin in it to secure it. He said the way it looked, I must have broken it at least a year or two before.

I don't remember breaking it the first time around, but I can tell you exactly what would have happened. I would have hurt my foot and said nothing because I didn't want to miss matches or even training and, eventually, it would have healed to a point where I could just carry on as normal. Let's just say my attitude hasn't changed much.

My rehab wasn't exactly textbook. When I could walk, I bypassed the next step and went straight to running. When I say I ran, I should point out that I was doing so in a full cast. It's quite a skill. I would even join in on matches in the playground at school. No joke, I used to kick goals with the cast on. Retrospectively, it's nothing short of a miracle I recovered at all, but, when I did, and I officially returned to training – cast free – my football had gone to a new level.

It gives me chills to think about how it could have gone the other way. I could have sabotaged my whole career. If you're recovering from an injury and it involves wearing a cast, I highly advise you don't follow my rehab programme.

Steven Gerrard is one of my all-time sporting heroes, and in his book he talks about how his career almost ended before it began. When he was nine, he was kicking around a football when in a freak accident he kicked a garden fork that was hidden in the grass, and it impaled his big toe. Doctors were talking about removing it. Were it not for the intervention of Liverpool's medical team – as he was already in the academy by then (crazy, I know) – he would have lost more than his toe. He would have lost his whole career and the sporting world would have been deprived of, in my view, not just one of the best footballers of all time but one of the sport's best leaders.

While my impact on the sporting landscape is only marginally less than that of Steven Gerrard – don't you agree? – it is no less humbling to realise you are only ever one poor decision away from ending everything.

I don't really know why but, when I returned to the game, I started to stand out from the pack – even I noticed it.

Maybe that cast, which was absolutely rank by the time I went to get it taken off, had special powers.

I began to dominate in both training and games. I was moved to midfield for the Under-16 county final, a position I don't ever remember playing prior to that game. We won comfortably and I was awarded man of the match. This was the first time in my life I left a game feeling as though I was clearly the best player on the pitch. It was like I was just doing as I pleased. It was weird, because I'm sure I'd had great games before then, but I just wouldn't allow myself to feel good about them. I had never let my inner dialogue reflect too positively on myself. But the proof was in the pudding and I was clearly pulling away from the group.

My opinion of myself was starting to change.

It was around this time that I was given the chance to rectify my mistake from years earlier and join the school's senior team. When they asked this time, it was a resounding yes from me. I ended up being appointed captain that year. We made the semi-finals of the Leinster schools championship, and drew with St Mel's of Longford. The replay was memorable for reasons on and off the field.

Despite the fact we lost, I had a great game. I kicked four frees and a point from play (five points total). I was the designated long-range free-kick taker, and I was on song.

I wasn't the only future AFL player on the field. Michael Quinn, who would go on to play for Essendon, was the main man for St Mel's. He ended up playing for the Bombers for two seasons. He was phenomenal that day, scoring two goals and two points (eight points total) and he basically won the match for St Mel's. After a tense contest, though, things boiled over after the final whistle.

I've never been one to fight, either on a football field or a night out, I was always the one trying to break up scuffles. My first and only melee was in primary school when an older student took my tennis ball. I know – I couldn't believe it either. A crime truly worthy of fighting over.

We were kicking the ball against the wall at lunch-time and he took it. I put him in a headlock and tried to hold him as hard as I could but, unfortunately, he kept punching me in the face. I feel like I won as he spent the whole fight in a headlock, but he did bust my lip open pretty badly so the judges, my classmates, were split on a decision.

Given my almost divine good looks, I couldn't risk any more damage to the money-maker as it seemed likely, nah almost inevitable, that I would end up being a world-famous model. After the tennis ball incident, I decided to retire from fighting with immediate effect. And although I never became a model, I think this was a wise business decision on my behalf. I haven't been involved in a fight since.

However, in that semi-final, one of my teammates, who had not retired from fighting yet – he was at his peak – decided to fire up at the end of the match. He's such a lovely guy but he was a real hothead when he was younger, so he started a fight and got a red card. The only way to break up an on-field fight without making it worse is to extract your own teammates. That was usually my role. If you try to drag the opposition guys out, you're just instigating it.

Even though I dislike confrontation, I knew I had to get involved. In my mind that would show great leadership. I eventually managed to de-escalate it, but it took a while to disperse. The atmosphere wasn't great in the change room after, but I felt like I'd played my part. I was just devastated that we had lost. I've never, ever, been okay with losing – anything. In fact, I think I've got worse as I've got older.

I have also, perhaps counterintuitively, become more hot-headed as I've got older. I have less patience with guys who want to act like idiots on the field than I've ever had. Especially because so many of the AFL's modern-day provocateurs only act that way because they know there's virtually no chance of retaliation. Players today won't risk suspension or public scrutiny by whacking anyone, so players who in years gone by would have been too cowardly to upset anyone are now strutting around like Billy Big Balls thinking they can do as they please. This does my head in, but I digress.

After the Leinster semi-final, things began to move fast.

As I said, I had never gone to trials for the intercounty team but, around this time, my old man got a tap on the shoulder from Brendan Delaney, a work colleague of his, who was one of the team selectors for the Under-16 county team. Brendan asked Daddy if he would bring me to Laois training.

Up I went, and I think I only played a couple of games at Under-16 level before I was elevated onto the Under-18 side.

In 2007, we opened our minor campaign against Kilkenny. For those reading who aren't fortunate enough to call themselves Irish, let me explain. Kilkenny is a wonderful hurling county, one of the best ever, but, quite frankly, they are a deplorable footballing county. I mean awful. We did, however, prepare for them diligently, as we did for every team. With professionalism and attention to detail. We were ready for them to at least put up a fight and, maybe, they were hoping to catch us off guard and cause an upset.

That didn't happen. We thrashed them by 26 points (4–20 to 0–06) and, for my Australian friends, that's about as big a margin as you're ever likely to see in a game of football. But the real stuff was about to begin.

We played Dublin next. After normal time, it was a draw, and I had been subbed off late in the piece. I was shattered. I don't think I'd ever been subbed off before, but there you have it. When the game went into extra-time, I was subbed back on. That doesn't happen often, but I made the most of it. The scores were tied after extra-time.

We defeated Dublin comfortably in the replay when I was redeployed as an attacking half-back. Having played most of the championship at centre-forward, this, at the time, felt like a slight demotion. But the switch may have played an integral part in getting me drafted to the AFL.

That year, we went on to win the minor Leinster title, beating Carlow in the final. It was during this Leinster final that I scored what would turn out to be the most important point of my life.

Early in the game, I caught one of our own kickouts well inside our defensive half, and I just took off. I managed to sprint away from a couple of would-be tacklers, carrying the ball the entire way up to the opposing 13-metre line, before spinning away from one final attempted tackle and kicking it over the bar. It was a lovely point, even if I do say so myself, but I had no idea at the time just how much that point was going to change my life.

We defeated Roscommon in the All-Ireland quarter-final and were drawn to face Derry in the semi-final.

Derry was leading for most of the game that day. From half-back, I managed to push forward and get a goal, followed up by a 45 (a free kick from 45 metres). My offensive game was firing but, as we entered added time at the end of the match, we were still four points adrift. Nothing but a goal was going to get us back into this.

I remember rolling forward and receiving a looping hand pass from Conor Meredith, another player who would try his hand at an AFL career, spending two years with North Melbourne. I stepped inside the chasing Derry defender and beat two more in front of me to kick it into the top right-hand corner of the net. It went in as fast as a bullet, so much so the goalkeeper barely moved, he had no chance. It ended up being goal of the year, and it was easily the best goal I'd ever scored in Gaelic football, at a pretty handy time too.

My teammate Donal Kingston scored a brilliant individual point moments later to force the game to a replay.

In the replay, I was selected in the forward half, but it wasn't our day. We allowed Derry to score a few sloppy goals in the first half, and we gave ourselves too much work to do in the second half.

Immediately after the game, I was awarded the Bobby Miller Man of the Match for my performances over the two semi-final games.

Not long after the minor intercounty campaign had drawn to a close, we played in a blitz-style tournament with the Portlaoise minors in Dunboyne in County Meath.

If the Under-16 county final a couple of years earlier had been the beginning of my journey towards self-belief, then this tournament was the destination.

There were Under-18 teams from all over Ireland, and the legendary Meath football coach Seán Boylan was there too. It was a 13-a-side format – I remember that because it felt like there was always space for me to run into, I had so much freedom.

This tournament capped off what had been a trans-formative season for me. I was playing in the midfield, catching kickouts and running the length of the field to score. We absolutely destroyed every team we played that day, and won the tournament outright. I was given the Player of the Tournament award, and it's no exaggeration to say that I'd arrived. This was who I was now – a bona fide athlete. Most importantly, I believed it.

My former coach, Mick Lillis, who was in charge at the time, also recalls this tournament as the standout moment of my junior career. By now, he was completely convinced that I had the potential to achieve something special. Of course, doing that on the other side of the world wasn't on his radar – or mine – just yet.

A few days later, our house phone rang. What I didn't know, as I walked into the hallway to answer it, was that this phone call would change my life forever.

CHAPTER 3

Making It Onto
the (Heat) Map

WHEN I ANSWERED THE PHONE, I THOUGHT IT was a journalist from the North calling about the Derry game, and my mind was searching for context. The last accent I expected to hear was an Australian one. But that's exactly what it was.

It was Gerard Sholly, a talent scout representing Carlton.

Back then we had a landline in the hallway, no caller ID, no country code that could hint at who this caller was. After watching me play, he had worked hard to get my number, going through the phone book (old school) and making a list of Tuohys. Luckily for him, our house was the first one he called.

'We're organising a draft combine in Limerick. Do you want to come?' he said.

My fellow county man Colm Begley was already playing AFL with the Brisbane Lions, which I thought was the coolest thing ever. He was living the dream, and all of us boys wanted to be like him. I had heard murmurs there were Aussies around, looking for players, but I'd had no idea they'd been looking at me. I started to wonder if it was a prank. Had one of my friends called thinking this was a genius gag?

No, this seemed legit. My Portlaoise mates would not be this skilled at an Australian accent. I tried to act cool on the phone but, internally, I was freaking out. I immediately agreed to go to the trial. As soon as I put the phone down, I realised two things. Firstly, I barely knew what was involved in Aussie Rules. Secondly, I was now laser-focused on making this opportunity a reality. At 17, I'd found my direction: I wanted to play AFL.

After sitting the Leaving Certificate earlier in the year, I had been planning to study at Carlow Institute of Technology. I was going to study IT but had very little interest in the course. This phone call ensured I had even less interest – if that was possible. Performing well in that combine and getting an AFL team to sign me was my singular goal. Everything else was now on the backburner.

I walked into the kitchen after I put down the receiver. There was a feeling in my stomach that I can only imagine is akin to what it would feel like to win the lotto. You believe it's happening, but you're struggling to put a new context on everything. It was like butterflies, with a heart flutter on the side.

I looked around our kitchen. Mammy was pottering around. My brain was struggling to comprehend this. I couldn't actually say anything for a few seconds. Everything looked the same but, for me, everything had changed.

I eventually got the words out.

'I have an Aussie Rules trial. They're interested in me,' I said in a muted tone that didn't match my internal constitution. I was trying to reorder my world as I knew it.

I'm sure Mammy was too. She looked at me with eyes desperate to show support and excitement, but with an undeniable and underlying realisation and sadness because of what this could mean.

I'll always be grateful that she masked those emotions as much as she could and led with support. It would have been difficult, but she knew I was desperate to be a professional athlete.

I assumed that Gerard's interest had peaked when I scored that goal (of the year) against Derry, but it was actually that point I kicked in the Leinster final against Carlow that garnered attention. For him, that was enough. He said he only needed to see one moment to know. He wasn't looking for a ready-made AFL player, he was looking for a project, someone a club could work with and mould into an AFL player. He said the reason he hadn't called straightaway was because he didn't want to cause a distraction while we were still in the competition.

There was around six months between that life-changing phone call and the combine itself. Back then, it felt like forever.

After Gerard's call, Daddy and I developed new TV habits. Every week, we would sit down to watch the AFL highlights. In Ireland, there was a short show with all the weekend's action. It was no *Match of the Day*, but we loved it.

Playing that game – being in those highlights one day – was all I could think about. I was obsessed with the AFL website too. They had goal heat maps for every match with coloured dots on the field to indicate where every major was kicked. If you hovered over the dots, you could see the name of the kicker. Because Gerard was scouting on behalf of Carlton at the time, I obviously started barracking for them. Brendan Fevola was the big-name star at the time and became my favourite player. He was their superstar forward and I monitored his stats obsessively.

Even back then, I had complete clarity on what I wanted to achieve. I loved Gaelic football and I loved my club, but the GAA was never going professional. Leaving it was the only way I could get paid to play sport. I wasn't thinking about what I was leaving behind, I was thinking about what could be in my future – if I could just make it happen.

I had a very short and simple road map to success. Part one: become an established AFL player. Part two: win a Premiership. Easy, right?

I was looking at the draft picks Carlton was getting and thinking, *Surely, they're only five years away from winning a flag?* Sorry, Carlton fans, I know this will hurt to read.

The draft combine was at the University of Limerick. The roster of players who went to try out turned into a who's who of Gaelic games. Dublin star Dean Rock topped the list. He would go on to win eight All-Irelands and three All-Stars (the equivalent of All-Australian awards) during his career. Then, there was Ciarán Sheehan from Cork, who would eventually become my teammate at Carlton – but not as soon as initially planned.

When we arrived, recruiters gave us a brief introduction to the sport and showed us a Sherrin (an Australian Rules football, the equivalent of an O'Neills – I had never seen one in real life before). Then, they ran us through the schedule and we were straight into it.

We had fitness tests in the morning, which I'm okay at, but not outstanding. It was pouring rain in the afternoon when we went out on the field to do skills. It was mucky and cold. If I just did well, I wouldn't have to experience this type of weather while playing again. Back then, I thought everywhere in Australia was sunny all of the time. I didn't know Melbourne actually has four seasons, and winter is definitely one of them.

The Sherrin was slippery, and I'd never kicked one before. *Not ideal*, I thought. I'd never kicked any form of oval-shaped ball. From Gaelic football to soccer, a round ball was all I'd ever known.

When we started, to my great surprise, it all came naturally. I've told you about my confidence issues in sport growing up, but even I could see that I was kicking the Sherrin more skilfully than my peers. In the end, the rain was beneficial as it increased the difficulty of the skills, but I had no problem adapting, regardless of how wet it got. I could tell the recruiters were impressed.

They singled me out. Along with one other player. Ciarán Sheehan, despite not being able to take part in the full day's testing due to an injury, had impressed sufficiently in his minor campaign with Cork to have been flagged as a top candidate already. We didn't know each other back then. Little did I know our journeys would be intertwined for years to come.

I didn't hear anything for a few days, which was long enough for me to wonder if I ever would. If I was home, I always stayed close to the phone. I didn't want to miss Carlton's call – I knew the combine had gone well.

A few days later, Gerard got in touch again. 'Would you like to go to Melbourne for a trial with Carlton?' he asked.

Would I what? Emmmmm, let me think about it – yes, yes I would!

I couldn't believe it. I was headed for Australia.

It took a few months to organise and, during that time, I was keen to show the Blues what I could offer. Mammy helped me put a DVD together with a highlights reel that we posted to the club. After what felt like forever, my ticket to Australia was booked. My first trial would take place in August 2008.

As much as my parents fully supported me, the reality of my departure hit us all when they were dropping me at the airport for that first flight to Melbourne.

Mammy was a mess. I was only going for a couple of weeks, but she knew what was coming down the line – that this could be the start of losing me to Australia, at least for a few years. She was sobbing so hard it broke my heart. I could barely look at her. She vowed that she'd never accompany me to Dublin airport again and, since that very first time, she never has.

I've learned that seeing your parents cry is one of the toughest parts of living abroad. Anyone who has lived away from home will understand this. People don't see their parents cry that often during their lifetime – at least, if you're lucky, you don't. But when you live away from home, not only do you see them cry, you also *make* them cry. This might happen once or twice a year, depending on how often you see them and then inevitably have to say goodbye.

My emotions were all over the shop. While in the pit of my stomach I felt sheer excitement for the opportunity that was on offer, the visual of my mum rendered inconsolable had rattled me.

But I was 18 and, when you're a teenage boy, you recover quickly. I'd checked in my bags and had that boarding card that said Melbourne on it in my hand. What could go wrong?

I'll tell you what – Heathrow airport. What a hellhole.

Anyone who has flown through Heathrow will know how insanely busy it is. It's especially frustrating having to stop there on the way from Ireland to Australia as it's just over an hour away and seems so unnecessary. And of all the airports in the world to make your way through, it is the most challenging.

I was doing my best to clear all of the security required and get to my boarding gate. But there were people everywhere and it was difficult to navigate. The screens were especially hard to decipher for this very young, green traveller who had never left the country on his own before, much less travelled to the other side of the world. It felt like I'd only just arrived at the airport when the massive screens showed a blinking 'Boarding' against my flight number. Not realising that boarding takes a long time, I went into panic mode.

'Are you okay?' a big burly security guard asked.

'Not really,' I said. 'I need to get to my gate, it says it's boarding soon and I can't miss it.'

This very kind security guy, who probably had more pressing things to do, took pity on me and walked me to the gate, reassuring me as we went that I had plenty of time. He wished me luck for my Australian adventure, and I was very grateful to him. Before long, I was on my way – for real this time.

When I finally got on the plane, all I could do was stare at the flight map. Australia looked like such a long way away. After my stopover in Dubai, I continued to monitor the map between naps until the tiny plane was over Australian land. *We'll be there any minute*, I thought.

I quickly learned just how big Australia is. The tiny plane diagram was hovering over Perth when I thought we were almost there. I had to watch it crawl over the continent for five more hours. I kept watching, and the closer we got to Melbourne on the map, the more excited I got.

Rod Ashman, who was a former player at the club and the player-welfare manager, picked me up at the airport and I stayed at his house that first night. I'll never forget waking up the following morning and thinking, *Wow, I'm here.*

Rod presented me with Special K for breakfast. I had never tried it before, but I said yes to be polite. I was starving so I ate it. At this stage, I was strictly a Rice Krispies and Coco Pops man – I wasn't exactly on the diet of a professional athlete. This Special K was going to take some getting used to, but if that's what footballers ate down here, then I would too … even if I had to force it down.

I'll never forget arriving at the club for the first time. I was expecting a slick, shiny, elite facility like the ones I had seen on TV when I watched the English Premier League. Let's just say that, back then, before the club was renovated, it was not like what I had seen on TV. In fact, it was an absolute shithole. I couldn't believe it when they gave me the tour, I was devastated. The club put me up in a hotel just across the road and, as I checked in that afternoon, I was generally underwhelmed by my day one experience.

My second day at the club involved another important introduction, and it was as disappointing as the facilities. I went to a café across the road to meet the head of football, Steven Icke. He asked me if I wanted a coffee. I was not a coffee drinker at the time but inexplicably said 'yeah'. Like the Special K episode, I just wanted to be polite. Then, he asked a question I didn't have an answer for.

'What would you like?' he said.

'A coffee,' I replied, although I thought we'd just discussed this.

'But what type of coffee?'

There were types?! My mind went blank. Clearly my face was blank too.

'How about a cappuccino,' he smiled.

I agreed. Even though I didn't have a fucking clue what a cappuccino was. Never mind a latte. Whatever that was, it seemed to be the coffee of choice for the suits who sat upstairs at the club and who had come over to officially welcome me to my trial.

When my cappuccino arrived, I hesitantly took a sip. It was vile, but, of course, I drank it all. It's funny to look back on because, pretty soon, I couldn't function without it. These days, I can't operate without two serves of that vile substance a day.

Apart from developing a coffee habit, I didn't get much from that first visit to Melbourne. I felt like the club hadn't organised much for me and I was left to my own devices a lot. I was just hanging around, observing, and it was really awkward.

My personality doesn't really lend itself to walking up to famous AFL players to introduce myself. I remember watching Brendan Fevola going about his business at the club, which was surreal after I had spent the last months hovering over that AFL.com.au heat map to learn about his goals. Chris Judd was there too; he had a real presence, and I was very aware of his standing in the game. And there I was, just hanging around on the sidelines, trying to drink coffee without vomiting.

When they did include me in training activities, it was a major highlight. One drill was particularly memorable. It was a handball drill with two groups of eight players competing against each other. The aim of the drill was to zigzag the ball up and down in a race to see who could do it the quickest. I was on Fev's team, and we won. He took great delight in sledging the other team when we did.

'We won, and we had an Irish guy on our team who has never even played AFL,' he laughed.

Fev seemed like a good egg. I was already a huge fan, so, for him to include me, even just to sledge his teammates, meant a lot. In Ireland, we only sledge people we like. I was disappointed that when I eventually started my first contract with the club, he had left for the Brisbane Lions.

I have great memories of those times we did cross paths. The man on that AFL.com.au heat map was even better in real life. If you're Australian and reading this book, Fev needs no introduction. If you're Irish and don't know a lot about him, you may remember him from an infamous incident involving a headlock in a Galway bar during the 2006 International Rules Tour. He was fun-loving. Although he would occasionally go a little too far with some of his off-field shenanigans, that hasn't stopped me being a big Fev fan to this day.

But, truthfully, other than getting to do a drill with Fev, I hated that first trip. I really hated it.

Despite those feelings, I was desperate for the chance at professional sport and wanted to sign up with the Blues as soon as possible. I was 18 and, when I got back to Ireland, I started my college course, but I was just biding my time.

The club was keen on Ciarán Sheehan and me starting our AFL journey together so that we could support each other, which was smart. But Ciarán had one year left at minor level (Under-18) and wanted to see it through, so our departure was delayed for a year. Instead of starting pre-season at the end of 2008 in preparation for the 2009 season, we would join the club 12 months on.

The next stint I did in Melbourne was almost a year later, in July 2009. It was a month-long trial, and it was much more enjoyable. This time, Ciarán travelled with me and we stayed with Greg Swann, the CEO of Carlton at the time. He had a lovely house and we stayed in a granny flat out the back. They even gave us a car. I was promised that I could use that car when I moved out permanently.

Ciarán was injured at the time so he couldn't train with the Victoria Football League (VFL) team – the Northern Bullants. He hurt his back while lifting weights in the gym, shortly after arriving in Melbourne. For those reading in Ireland, the VFL competition is a step below AFL, and every team has an affiliated side – the Blues VFL side was the Bullants. If you're dropped from AFL, that's where you go to play in a bid to impress and push for a return to the senior side. If you're coming back from injury, sometimes that's where you play your first match.

It was the perfect training ground for an Irish player trying to transition from Gaelic football to Aussie Rules, but it was intimidating turning up to that first session without Ciarán. Luckily for me, the team couldn't have been more welcoming. The one thing I had in my favour at those sessions was that I kicked well straightaway. It helped me blend in, which was all I wanted to do.

After our month-long stay, the club told us they wanted to sign us both. I was ecstatic.

I'll never forget getting my first official contract – a copy of it is framed in my house back home. Steven Icke flew over to Ireland, and I signed it in Lilly's pub in Portlaoise. Back then it was called Egan's. That venue would later end up being owned and run by one of my best mates, Kieran Lillis.

I remember calling my sister Naomi at work after I signed it. She cried. But she cries at all good news. It's a running gag in our family. She cried when I got my contract, when my kids were born, when I got engaged, when I won the Grand Final. She's so strong but she's a softie deep down. Good things make her cry, sad things just make her angry. Things are generally pretty good when Naomi's crying.

When I told my dad it was a done deal, he had one request. 'You can come home anytime you like but don't come home before we make our first trip out there to see you.'

Fair enough. That was booked for six months' time. At that point, I had no idea if I'd make it to that milestone. Given how much I had hated my first trip to Australia, I wasn't sure if I'd last long enough for my parents to avail themselves of the free flights the club had agreed to provide.

The GAA club threw a massive going-away party for me. Back then, when a player was recruited to Australia, clubs and counties who were losing their best players were often resentful. That wasn't the case with Portlaoise. They couldn't have been prouder. The last match I played for the club was an Under-21 game in Ratheniska, which we won. We played our great rivals, Stradbally, and it was fitting for my last official game before starting life as a professional athlete.

At the end of the match, my teammates presented me with a jersey to take to Australia. We were in our usual post-match huddle when they handed it over. I'm sure there were words said, but being so young and so excited to head to Australia, I've no idea what they were. It was all a big whirlwind.

They also planned a big night out, so I would remember – or forget as the case may have been – my last night out with the boys. They'd decorated the pub with balloons and banners. I've always felt like my former teammates and coaches revelled in my success as much as anyone. Having invested so much time into my development as a junior player, you might expect that some would feel animosity towards me for leaving. Not at all. They took pride in the fact that they were able to help one of their own achieve his dream. I don't think I could ever adequately repay Portlaoise GAA and all my coaches for what they did for me, but I plan on trying.

Let's just say not every player who signed an AFL contract got a friendly going-away do. Some counties were vehemently against Australian scouts poaching Gaelic football talent, and key figures in the game were campaigning for the International Rules Series to be cancelled, as they felt it was providing a shop window for Australian clubs. Of all the counties that resisted, Tyrone was very much up there.

Kyle Coney, who was a player for Tyrone and one of the standout minor footballers in Ireland around this time, signed for the Sydney Swans in 2008 on a two-year rookie contract. He went to Australia and did a few weeks of pre-season, made a trip home to visit family – and never returned after Christmas.

I've no doubt he would have been under huge pressure to stay at home and represent his club and county, and, of course, he would have been missing family too. That's a lethal festive cocktail. I'm sure the same was true for Ciarán Kilkenny, who went to Hawthorn Footy Club for a few weeks and also never returned after the Christmas break.

The thing about Gaelic football is that you play for the county that you're born in. You don't transfer. So, if a county loses a promising player, they can't just draft someone in. Around the time I was leaving, it became clear I was on track to make a major contribution to my club and to my county. They can't have been thrilled I was leaving. For them to react in the way that they did was impressive.

I was due to fly to Melbourne in late September 2009, and I was on cloud nine.

Kieran Lillis and I had planned an early-morning gym session. He was always up for doing extras and made for a great training buddy. I was asleep when the phone rang. It was early, too early to get up for our session, but when I saw his number pop up on my phone, I assumed he was calling to confirm. He wasn't one to cancel.

He wasn't doing either of those things.

He was calling to talk about our mutual friend, Jim Savage. Jim was studying at Galway university. 'Have you heard about Jim?' Kieran said.

'No,' I said. 'What about him?'

'He's gone. He's dead.'

Jim, who was just 20 years old, had taken his own life.

As far as we were concerned, he was the happiest person we knew. People wanted to be around him. He had the most infectious smile and was always making people laugh. It made no sense.

I'll never forget the wake. It was held in his house. Irish wakes are different to Australian wakes. In Ireland, the body of the deceased is laid out at home, so you can visit and pay your respects. I remember walking there with a group of friends. None of us knew what to say.

As soon as we turned the corner into the housing estate where we would see our friend, we burst into tears. The reality of what we were about to face hit us hard. I was too young to know how to process what had happened. My feelings crept up on me and hit me like a steam train. I left shortly after seeing him in his casket.

Jim was loved by everyone who'd ever had the privilege of meeting him. One of a kind, who's been sorely missed ever since.

When I look back on that time, it feels like a blur. I was too young to fully process what had happened. Or maybe I didn't want to. I just got on with things – I didn't know what else to do.

I wish I could say that was the last time I would see one of my friends laid out. It wasn't.

Soon after, I found myself back at Dublin airport, getting ready to leave for my first season as a professional athlete. I was alone.

Not long before my departure, Ciarán had decided to pull out. He'd had second thoughts about leaving Cork to pursue AFL. I had waited an extra year so that he could finish playing minor football and we could go together, but I'd now be travelling on my own anyway.

At the time, I felt like he had cost me a year of playing professional football. That extra year spent at home could have been used to adapt to training and come to terms with footy and life in Australia. Instead, I'd left Carlow IT to do a course in personal training that I would probably never use. I could have been 18 when I started my career, but I was now just months off turning 20. It felt like a waste to have waited for someone else and then end up going solo after all.

Now I'm older and wiser, I look at it very differently. For all I know, if I'd come out too young, I could have been injured or become terribly homesick. Instead, I was a 20-year-old starting my first professional season, and maybe that made a difference. I did my first pre-season at the end of 2009 and spent 2010 playing VFL (second tier to AFL). It was meant to be that way – for both Ciarán and me. At least it sure looks that way. Ciarán ended up winning an All-Ireland and returning to Carlton to play after the 2013 International Rules Series, so I'm sure he's happy with how things panned out too.

While airport departures are always tough, Mammy didn't come along this time, and I had mastered the screen situation at Heathrow. This time, my flight to Melbourne went as smoothly as it could. I was giddy with excitement.

I'll never forget the Carlton kitman 'Bulldog' giving me my first training kit. This was a huge moment – my first, free, professional training kit. The kit comprised of a backpack with a couple of training tops, shorts and socks. It was pretty minimal – but, to me, it was everything.

Unlike my two previous trips to Australia, I loved everything about my new life. I loved training with the boys, I loved being a professional athlete. It had always been my dream, and I was pleased that, despite hating the first trial and finding the second one okay at best, I was loving life.

Waking up every day and going to training was what I had always wanted, and now I was doing it. Training during the day felt like a luxury. In the GAA, because of its amateur status, players work or study during the day and then train in the evening. Often, it was cold and wet, and you were tired by the time you got on the field. I hated evening training. Now, it was all I had to do during the day. Bliss.

I spent a couple of months in pre-season training before heading back to Ireland for Christmas. Unlike many Irish players before me, I had no issue returning after the festive season. I couldn't wait for my first full season as a professional athlete.

Life was good apart from one major issue: transport.

Remember that car I talked about that the club promised when I arrived? They took it off me after a few weeks. I got a ticket for going through a red light, and that was that.

I got the ticket driving to post-match recovery in St Kilda, and I was petrified of being late. I also had no clue where I was going, so was diligently following a convoy of teammates' cars through traffic. The light was yellow at Wurundjeri Way next to Marvel Stadium when I followed Lachie Henderson through the intersection. Unfortunately, it was red when the camera snapped me. The club took me aside and told me off. I thought, *Okay, fine, lesson learned.* But when I returned after my Christmas holidays, they had taken the car away.

I wasn't earning much, so I was very relieved when my teammate Aisake Ó hAilpín offered me his backup car. It was a 97 Honda Civic and, if you drove it more than a kilometre, it overheated. Honestly, that car almost ended my AFL career before it began.

I remember on one occasion it broke down on Royal Parade, about 500 metres from the club. I had to wait for the engine to cool down so I could continue to drive to training. It would have been quicker to walk but I couldn't abandon that shitcan of a car. I was distraught and humiliated. There I was, standing on the side of the road, in my full Carlton kit, while other players happily, and unknowingly, drove past me to training. That piece of shit caused me so much heartache. I do remember Setanta, Aisake's brother, jokingly pitching the idea of renting the car for a weekly fee. I don't think the car survived long enough for payments to begin. It wasn't worth the price of a Melbourne latte, never mind a weekly fee.

Apart from the car-rental suggestion, Setanta and Aisake

were legends. They really looked after me in the early days. I spent a lot of time at their house, even when I was in Melbourne doing trials. They were loyal and would do anything for you. They were also super protective of each other, so it was good to be in their layer.

Setanta would talk about a hundred games being an incredible achievement for any Irish player. That was his goal at the time, and I'm sure he would have got there were it not for a bad knee injury towards the end of his career – an injury he suffered playing against Carlton after he switched to Greater Western Sydney (GWS) in 2012.

Money was tight in those early days. In spite of the fact that I had moved from the other side of the world, there was one perk enjoyed by my interstate teammates that I, ironically, didn't qualify for – the 'moving away from home allowance'.

My interstate colleagues were given a chunk of cash to set up their homes, buy furniture, a new TV, etc., but, despite moving hemispheres, I somehow wasn't eligible. I also couldn't study because of visa issues. There was a mandatory course first-year players had to do and, upon completion, most players would receive a payment of about two grand. They wouldn't pay me that either, so I refused to do the course, which was some sort of leadership induction-type thing. My teammates said I didn't miss anything. It's fair to say that, back then, we weren't looked after as well as players are today.

On the field, and away from the cash-strapped Honda Civic situation, things had been going pretty well. Then, I was handed a major reality check. Having played for the first few games of the 2010 VFL season, I was dropped to the VFL reserves (which doesn't exist now, and I wish it hadn't existed back then either).

Looking back, being dropped was a good thing because, in the reserves, I dominated. But when you're in that league it's like playing in Gaelic football's 'Junior B' championship. It's terrible. That was hard to swallow because it felt like a very long way from the AFL. It was also the first time in my life I had been demoted in this way. Ultimately, it was good for me and I was back in the VFL in a matter of weeks. Let's just say I had a newfound urgency to make sure I stayed there for the rest of my first season.

It was early in my career when I learned just how far I was from home. There's nothing like receiving bad news to emphasise the geographical reality.

It was my first season with the club in 2010, and I was busy trying to hone my skills in the VFL.

One evening, I'd returned from training and was sorting through my dirty kit (back then it was washed by my host family – just like Mammy used to) and wondering what would be served up for dinner. Yes, I was spoiled.

I got a text from Daddy: 'Are you free to talk?'

Straightaway this set off alarm bells. He would usually just call me or ask for what he wanted via text, so I knew something was wrong. I went into my room and sat on the bed waiting for his call.

The host family I was staying with were the De Bolfos – wonderful people. I had really landed on my feet with them. Tony De Bolfo is a footy historian who's written books on the history of Carlton Football Club. A diehard Blues fan and an all-round great bloke. They lived along a row of terraced houses in Preston and owned two properties next to each other, which meant that Pete Labi, another first-year player from Papua New Guinea, and I lived in one house by ourselves, while the rest of the De Bolfo family lived in the other.

It was a perfect setup, and I was happy to have their support after I had chatted to Daddy.

'I've got Parkinson's,' Daddy said.

'What?' I couldn't believe what I was hearing.

In typical Daddy fashion, he immediately followed it up with reassurance. 'Don't worry, it's not hereditary.'

As if that's the first thing I was thinking! As if my initial reaction would be, 'Oh you've got Parkinson's, does that mean I will get it?'

That conversation sums up Daddy, though. Always thinking of his kids ahead of him. He continued to play the situation down so I wouldn't worry. If you didn't know what Parkinson's was and you were relying on him to educate you, you'd think it was no more than a cold.

I was devastated. Straightaway I went online to try to learn a little more about it. I'd heard about it, but I had no idea what it involved.

Is it curable? What are the effects over time? What does the treatment look like? That was my Google search history that evening.

If you've grown up close to your father, you'll have thought the same as me – that your old man is invincible. This was the first time I had to confront the reality that he wasn't.

My siblings quickly followed up to see if I was okay. They knew it would be hard to hear when I was so far away from home. And, of course, I said I was fine. It was him I was worried about. I felt very grateful I was living with the De Bolfos. They were a great support to me and did a brilliant job as my pseudo-family at the time.

For a long time, the best form of treatment for Daddy was medication. He developed a tremor, which was mild initially but got worse over time. After years of strong medication, he had surgery in October 2021.

Deep brain stimulation (DBS) is a neurosurgical procedure that uses implanted electrodes and electrical stimulation to treat movement disorders associated with Parkinson's. In reality, for Daddy, that meant after months of planning and hours of MRIs, you get wheeled into the theatre at say 8 a.m. with the aim of being out of surgery at 5 p.m. It's nerve-racking, as it is one of those rare brain surgeries where you have to be awake during the procedure. That's right, you are completely conscious for a large part of the surgery.

My family didn't fill me in on these specifics at the time. All I knew was that the operation was due to start at around 9 p.m. Australian time, so I went to bed praying I'd wake up to good news.

I made myself go to bed early. My mother did not have that luxury. The surgery went on longer than expected, which must have been awful for her as she waited in the hospital. The procedure was more complex than expected, but it went well. After a marathon 11-hour surgery, Daddy was in recovery.

When I first heard about his diagnosis, I did what I always did. While I confided in my host family, I didn't tell anyone at the club. Footy always provided a distraction for me. I just got on with things. I didn't know it at the time, but this would become a habit. And not necessarily a positive one. 'Just shut the fuck up and get on with it' was my new-found stategy for dealing with adversity.

Even though I'd spent all of 2010 in the VFL, and a few weeks in the VFL reserves, the club's big hitters were welcoming. Chris Judd, who was just about the biggest name in the game at the time, was always up for a chat, no matter who you were.

I'll say it again. If you're Australian, you don't need any education on Chris Judd. If you're Irish and unfamiliar with

Juddy, trust me when I say he was a big deal. At the time of my arrival, he had already won just about everything there is to win in the game and, by the time he retired, he had added plenty more accolades to his CV.

Tony De Bolfo had written another book about the history of the club, and he gave me a special edition as a gift. I brought it to the club and sheepishly approached Chris to ask if he would sign it.

'Would you mind?' I said timidly, holding a sharpie.

I had no idea what the correct etiquette was for stuff like this. I mean, as a VFL player, was I even allowed to approach Chris?

But he turned to me with a wide smile and said, 'Of course I can. For my favourite new player, I'll do anything'.

That was Chris all over. Despite his standing in the game, Juddy had no airs or graces about him, and that never changed.

After spending a year in the VFL, I went home to visit family and play for Portlaoise. After the worry of Daddy's diagnosis, I was relieved that I couldn't see any change in him. If I hadn't already known he had Parkinson's, I wouldn't have been able to tell.

Of course, Carlton didn't know I was playing club football. I wasn't lying to them … I was just omitting some details.

I was happy with my first year at the Blues and confident about what the future held. My family and friends loved hearing stories about what it was like living the dream, getting paid to play.

As usual, I went to the first training session at the club after arriving home. All of my 'Town' teammates welcomed me back with open arms when I joined them on Tuesday for training. One of those teammates was a neighbour of mine, Peter McNulty.

Peter was a top footballer and had been for a long time. He was part of the Laois minor team that won the All-Ireland and everyone expected him to have a long and successful career as a senior intercounty player. We had grown up together; he lived just 100 metres down the road on Summerhill Lane.

Our little lane wasn't just home to Peter and myself, but also to Colm Byrne, who was full-back on the Laois senior team that won the Leinster title in 2003. Byrney had always treated me well when I played for the senior Portlaoise team. If you were a Summerhill Lane man, Colm had your back and that was that. We were proud of the fact that our lane had produced some top players. We were a tight group and I loved seeing those boys at training.

Peter was in top form and full of chat. There was nothing off with the conversation. I've played it over and over in my mind, but I didn't sense that anything was wrong.

On Thursday evening, there was no sign of Peter at

training. We didn't think anything of it. When he wasn't at training on Saturday morning, again, we didn't question it. It wasn't unusual for players to miss a couple of sessions here and there – he was probably just busy.

On Sunday morning, Kieran Lillis and I were walking around the shops in Newbridge when Shaun Byrne, Colm's brother, approached us.

'Have you heard about Peter?' he said.

'Heard about what?'

'He was found dead in his house this morning by his brother, Malachy.'

Peter had died suddenly. It was just a year after we'd lost Jim.

I try not to think about his wake, if I can. Those who knew Peter will attest to the fact he was always extremely well groomed. There was never a hair out of place and he loved a smart suit. Dapper 24/7 was our Peter. To see him lying in his suit in a coffin at such a young age was more than I could take.

Clubs from all over the county attended his funeral. Players from opposition clubs in their team colours lined the entrance to the church, forming a guard of honour as the hearse approached. Seeing our mortal enemies on the field making this gesture was poignant. It was testament to the lasting impact Peter had made on the football community in Laois. Peter's loss is still felt to this day. Gone far too young. Laois, Portlaoise and Summerhill Lane will never be the same again.

When I returned to Australia at the start of 2011, I brought a tie that Peter's brother Malachy had given me. I've kept that tie with me through changing circumstances and a fair few house moves.

One of those house moves was just after I returned to Melbourne. I had decided it was time to leave my host family, after spending my first year at Carlton with them, and go out on my own. But I still kept residence within the Blues family. I moved in with my teammate, Levi Casboult, who I had become really good friends with. His sister, Melissa, moved in too. We lived in a tiny townhouse on Melville Road in Brunswick West, and we loved it.

I started the year in the VFL and hit a major performance milestone in round one against Bendigo – my first ever 30+ possession game. For the benefit of Irish readers, I should explain that a possession means I've got my hands on the football. It's probably the most quoted stat in the game, other than goals, and anything over the 30 mark is considered elite. I continued to trend upwards and build confidence, and it was being noticed. I was continuously featuring in the 'best player' list each week. However, I still wasn't getting selected and I was becoming restless. Setanta Ó hAilpín, who I think it's fair to say didn't see eye-to-eye with our coach, Brett Ratten, or Ratts for short, was convinced that the coach wasn't in favour of the 'Irish experiment'.

I was really close to Setsy and his brother Aisaike; they looked after me like a brother. They never left me out and made sure I always had someone to socialise with. I owe both of them a lot for how kind to me they were at a time in my career when I needed some help and guidance. I appreciate everything they did for me.

However, at that time, Setanta felt as though Aisake had never been given a shot at AFL because Ratts didn't care much for Irish recruits. That was how it felt at the time, but, in hindsight, I'm sure this wasn't the case, and I have subsequently developed immense respect for Ratts but, back then, I took this on board. After all, I wasn't getting selected – I had no evidence to the contrary.

At least I didn't have to wait for my debut to have my first taste of playing on the MCG (Melbourne Cricket Ground is its full title, but everyone knows it as the MCG or 'the G'). For Irish readers who may not be familiar with the MCG, it holds the equivalent majestic status to Croke Park. It's where the Grand Final is held every year (except during a couple of Covid interrupted years) and can hold 100,000 fans. Playing there was an honour I was keen to experience.

Weeks before I played my first senior game, I was named as an emergency for a match against the Swans in Sydney. Being an emergency is the worst because you only get to play in exactly that situation, an emergency. So if a player gets injured in the warm-up, you get into the squad by default. You fly to the game with the team (if it's interstate) and when everyone makes it to the start, unscathed, you just sit there and watch, like a spectator. On this occasion, I was desperate to return to Melbourne because our VFL side were playing against the Greater Western Sydney (GWS) Giants at the MCG. It was the year before they entered the competition, so it meant their big-name recruits were playing.

I was desperate to experience playing there because, at that point, I had no idea how many times it would happen. Now, it looked like I wasn't going to be there for my first scheduled match at this hallowed stadium, playing for the Northern Bullants against Greater Western Sydney. I remember saying to Alan Richardson, who was an assistant at Carlton at the time, that I needed to go back and play on the G in case there were not too many opportunities in my future. He told me there would be plenty. I appreciated him saying that, as it carried weight. He had been a development coach with the Collingwood Magpies – the Pies – when Marty Clarke, another Irish footballer, was there. He had a fair idea what was required to make the transition.

My worries turned out to be for nothing, and I did get back to Melbourne in time for the MCG game.

Israel Folau was playing for GWS then. His move to the AFL was a huge story. He had been a superstar for Melbourne Storm in rugby league before switching codes. AFL ended up being a stopgap between his rugby league and well-documented rugby-union career. Even back then he was a huge name, so it was cool to play against him.

There we were, on the MCG – a former rugby league player and a former Gaelic footballer – just trying to establish ourselves in the AFL. It's fair to say my transition attracted way less scrutiny than his. Because of his profile, every move he made was documented in the press. He didn't dominate that day, which for a guy who is so athletically gifted was a surprise. It turned out that AFL wasn't for him.

The week before I finally debuted, we played against the Box Hill Hawks. Fortuitously, my parents were visiting at the time and were at that game. Yet again, I was dominant and even managed to kick a goal. I remember thinking after that match, *If I don't get selected now, I don't know what else to do.*

That performance convinced Ratts I was ready. But my good friend and housemate Levi also contributed to the club's decision – though not in the way that you'd think.

For the most part, our household was running well. Levi's sister Melissa was a nurse and had a stabilising effect on the home. We were gradually developing our cooking skills too, although it must be said, cooking is not one of my strong points. My repertoire consisted of meat and vegetables, some pasta dishes and my favourite and an absolute staple at the time: apricot chicken. We were especially proud of that dish. Not because we made it from scratch, of course not. We used a jar of Chicken Tonight sauce, or something like that. I shouldn't boast but the dish evolved to a level including – wait for it – vegetables. Groundbreaking stuff.

It wasn't this domestic bliss that helped ensure my progression to the next stage of my career, but a Saturday night out, weeks before my eventual debut.

Let's just say the night out was big and I woke up in a house, and bed, that was not my own. We had recovery at 8 a.m. so, as any diligent young footballer who is trying to get selected to play senior football would do, I got up early to do the 'Tram of Shame'. It's different to the 'Walk of Shame', as public transport is very good in Melbourne and trams are effective for those early-morning trips when you wake up without your car. The only issue was, after making the effort to get up early and doing an extremely hungover tram trip, when I arrived at my house I was greeted by an empty carport. *Fuck, how am I going to get to training now?*

Levi had taken my car to the club. He had assumed I'd go straight there. This was in the days before Uber. I'm not sure how I got there, maybe by taxi. But I was late, very late.

Levi had just been promoted to the senior list and had more or less been told that he would be playing that following weekend. But after the car mix-up and the subsequent disclosure about the reason for my lateness, coupled with the revelation that a group of us had been out drinking (which wasn't against the rules, but being late because of going out certainly was), the club informed Levi that he had fucked up, we all had, and as a result he wouldn't be playing AFL that week.

I don't know if he would have been selected that week or if it was just the coach's way of making him feel even worse, but either way it sucked.

This sliding-doors moment had unfortunate ramifications for him, which is sad, as he had woken up in his own bed and didn't deserve it.

He remained in the VFL, but got injured the following week in a match where he should have been playing AFL. His injury meant that I was promoted to the senior list. It still took a few more weeks before I was selected, but the important thing was to be elevated to the senior list. We still laugh about how our big night out, and him borrowing my car, contributed to my debut. When you get promoted to the senior list, you know your debut is just a matter of time.

Carlton was a military operation back then. If something like that happened to a young player at Geelong, they would be more understanding and take a slightly more caring approach. I mean, we both did our best to make it to recovery, and we had been permitted to go out the night before. Things just went horribly wrong – or horribly right – on my night out. But it could have been worse. If I'd still had Aisake's Honda Civic, neither of us would have made it to recovery – ever.

In the week building up to the AFL round-11 clash against Port Adelaide, the coach called me. When the coach calls, it can only be one of two things. You're either playing or you're sacked. They don't call for a chat. It was the halfway point of the regular home-and-away season, and I had been starting to lose patience. But it was finally happening.

In my debut game, we hammered Port Adelaide. I was the sub. Michael Jamison got injured in the first quarter – he rolled his ankle – and I was told to get ready to go on, but he ended up playing until almost the end of the third quarter, which resulted in me stressing for an hour and a half about the fact I was about to go on. I had used up so much nervous energy by the time I walked out onto the field that I was wrecked already.

I played really well in that last quarter, but my first touch ever in AFL was memorable for all the wrong reasons. I decided to bounce the Sherrin on the run and it went straight over my head. Literally, not metaphorically. Yep. *Oh fuck*, I thought. *Is this an omen for the rest of my career?*

Other than the Sherrin bouncing over my head, though, I was reasonably pleased with my debut. I ended up getting my hands on the footy a few times in my short time on the field and felt good about my performance, except, of course, for that first bounce.

I was selected to start the following week, and I kicked my first goal. We were playing the Brisbane Lions, and we were hammering them. In the final quarter, I was running down the far wing when Nick Duigan passed it to me. You always remember who gave you those early goal assists. I was 55 metres out and I played on. I backed myself, but the kick wasn't my best. It wasn't a shank, but it wasn't clean. It was definitely a goal though. The adrenaline coursing through my body at the thought of that first AFL goal propelled the ball around 10 rows back into the crowd.

Now, when you're thrashing a team, it's not cool to celebrate your goals. For that reason, I decided on a very muted reaction. However, my teammates had other ideas. Every one of them got around me. I'll never forget that feeling. I didn't expect them to do that for me. I didn't realise it at the time, but teammates are always willing you to that first goal. I've watched countless teammates kick their first since then, and swarmed them in celebration when they've achieved it. It's always a special feeling for the team, and a real mood lifter.

Not only had I played my second game, but I'd finally made it onto the heat map. Remember the one I used to obsess over on AFL.com.au? The one that showed the goal scorers? I was finally on the map.

CHAPTER 4

International
Man of Football

I'VE LED WITH THE HIGHLIGHTS OF MY FIRST AFL season but, don't get me wrong, there were lowlights too. It was a steep learning curve.

One rather innocuous match-review meeting has stayed with me to this day. When I say it was innocuous, it would have been to my teammates, but not to me.

In the aftermath of a loss against St Kilda, we gathered in the club theatrette. They brought a piece of video footage up on screen. St Kilda had managed to take the footy from deep in their back half, moving it seamlessly all the way through our defence, for a goal. Not ideal, obviously, and the coach wanted us to learn from it.

And as we surveyed the video footage, who was stood right in the middle of the ground by himself as all of this was happening? Me. *Shit*, I thought.

Ratts turned to the group and asked, 'What could we have done better here?'

I knew I was heavily implicated in this passage of play and I needed to make a decision on whether or not I owned up to it, while hoping he wouldn't single me out. I also didn't know if I had done anything wrong, so why draw attention to myself?

It's not easy when you're new in an environment like that. You're sitting in a room with some of the biggest names in the game; some real legends like Chris Judd and Kade Simpson would be looking at you and wondering if you knew what you were doing. I should point out that senior players like Chris and Kade did everything they could to make me feel comfortable, but it was still a daunting environment.

Should I risk speaking up?

For better or worse, I decided to answer with what can only be described as bald honesty.

'That's me in the middle, Ratts,' I sheepishly replied. 'And, to be honest, I'm still not sure if I did the right thing. I was trying to cover as much space as possible, but I'm honestly not sure what you want me to do here.'

I was relieved to have got it off my chest. But I braced myself for the reaction.

Ratts was brilliant.

Not only did I not cop a spray but I got a pat on the back – one for being so honest and another for making what he also thought was the right decision in covering a dangerous space. He went on to say that he understood how difficult those decisions are and he added that players don't have the benefit of pressing the pause button to look at the game in slow motion.

Ratts supported me and, from then on, I knew that if I didn't understand something or I wanted to ask something or just admit I was still learning, he was not only okay with that, he was encouraging it. He probably didn't even realise the effect that moment had, but it was significant for me. Maybe he wasn't as opposed to the 'Irish experiment' as Setanta Ó hAilpín had thought.

That year, the team played Essendon in the elimination final and thrashed them by 62 points. I was an emergency for that game but as soon as it started I drove to Port Melbourne to play in the VFL. I got there at quarter-time and played well, kicking a goal.

Because of that performance, I was named as a sub for the semi-final against the West Coast Eagles in Western Australia. Not only did I play in the first final of my AFL career, I also kicked one of my all-time favourite goals: an intercept mark and a goal kicked from the 50. We ended up losing by three points, but it had been a massively successful debut season, and I knew I could do more in 2012.

That semi-final goal was brought up in my end-of-season review with Brett Ratten. He talked about how impressed he had been with my performance coming on as a sub. Because I'd felt like I could have debuted earlier than I did, and because of Setanta's defensiveness about his brother's career and belief that Ratts had a bias against Irish footballers, I'd developed the idea in my head that Ratts didn't like me. But I was certain now that that wasn't the case. The way he talked to me and encouraged me in that meeting made me think he was actually a fan.

Setanta ended up leaving Carlton at the end of 2011 to join Greater Western Sydney. While he might have temporarily coloured my view of the coach, I'll always be grateful to him for everything he did to help me settle in at the Blues. He guided me through those first two years in the system, and I'll always be thankful he did.

2011 had already been a dream come true but, if possible, it was about to get better: I got selected to play for Ireland in the International Rules Series.

I had to attend a trial at Carton House to secure my spot in the side. I was at home visiting family in September having had only played 11 games of AFL, so I wasn't an automatic selection. The International Rules Series was a really big deal back then and I'd grown up watching it, so I was desperate to play. When I got in, I was ecstatic.

Those two weeks were probably the best two weeks of my life. I got out of a training trip to Abu Dhabi and Dubai with Carlton so I could play. While my teammates were getting absolutely smashed and doing altitude training, I was on a glorified piss-up. But what a piss-up it was. As my teammates did 6 a.m. wrestling sessions on the beach, I was doing 6 a.m. sambuca shots with my Irish teammates.

One of the best nights/days out was with Kerry's own Kieran Donaghy. We had met at the Carton House trials weeks earlier. Donaghy was at the peak of his powers for Kerry at the time, and I was impressed with how he included me in everything. We bonded straightaway. Kieran didn't have to look after me but, right from the start, he was generous with his time. When I made the squad, he never let me out of his sight. He always ensured I was part of the festivities.

We won the first test at Etihad Stadium (now known as Marvel) in Melbourne by 44 points and it was quite the weekend of celebrating. I enjoyed playing against my Carlton teammate Mitch Robinson as much as I enjoyed representing my country. We decided to go head-to-head early on. He wanted to wrestle me and we engaged in an affectionate little tussle. The photo of that tussle is one of my favourites from that match.

Melbourne's Brad Green was the captain of the Australian team, and I didn't like him, probably because he had played soccer when he was young and he kicked a Gaelic football very well. He would always sledge me when the Blues played the Dees (his usual team), so there was history.

He was a typical forward. When they're playing well and kicking goals, they love to tell you all about it. Sometimes, they will try to get in your head by saying things like, 'I want Tuohy, please match him up on me', just so you know that they think you're playing badly, while they're crushing it. As these things go with me, though, when he later joined Carlton as an assistant coach, I loved him.

You'd think that because of how often I transitioned from hating people I've never met off-field to really liking them when I did, that I might stop judging people solely on how they act on the field. But, no, that's never changed. And as long as I play any form of sport, I will continue to dislike people I barely know – based on extremely limited interactions on the field, thank you very much.

This is the story of my career. Irrational hatred of other teams and players motivates me. It always has.

One of the nights out in Melbourne after that first game, I ended up crashing on the couch in Donaghy's room. Mine had been taken over by a teammate with a newfound friend, shall we call them.

Kieran was good enough to offer his couch – not that I used it for long. We only got in at 3 a.m.-ish and by 6 or 7 a.m., Kieran was pitching the idea of heading back to the pub, and I thought, *Sure, why not?* Off we went. It was very early, but that was no issue for Kieran and myself.

The door of P.J. O'Brien's – the Irish bar nearest us – was wide open, and so inviting, and we assumed it was open when we walked in. It wasn't. There was a cleaner inside, but he didn't seem to care that we were back and looking for refreshments – he just kept going about his business, while we helped ourselves to a couple of bottles. After we finished those, we settled in for a couple more.

While the cleaner looked like he was okay with our early-morning presence on his shift, maybe he wasn't as complicit as we thought. Soon after, the manager – whom the cleaner must have called, and fair enough – walked in. He was remarkably calm about the fact we had opened his bar and started serving ourselves. I've always assumed he recognised Kieran, as most Irish people do. Perhaps he just chalked it down to harmless devilment from the Kerryman but, either way, he wasn't too upset. He did insist that we cease trespassing on the premises, though. We happily agreed to leave without incident.

Just for the record, we did leave $20 on the bar for our drinks because, although we were acting like raging alcoholics, we were raging alcoholics with a conscience.

This whole encounter did not deter Kieran. We continued our pub crawl and, eventually, ended up at a bar that is now known as Ponyfish Island. It's right in the middle of the Yarra River, nestled against one of the pillars holding up the footbridge to Flinders Street station in Southbank.

Everything was a little blurry to us at this point, but we were enjoying our day nonetheless. We were doing well considering the lack of sleep, but we felt, in our own minds, that our bender was successful. That was until it wasn't. We were sitting there with a bottle of Corona, when Donegal's Neil McGee turned up. It's always dangerous when someone fresh, or at least fresher than you are, joins a day out like this. Now, I love Neil and he was great craic. When he joined us and wandered over to the bar, I naturally assumed he was going to grab a beer – or maybe even a cider – something easy on the stomach, you know, to ease his way back into the day. He wasn't.

The fucker came back with a tray full of tequila shots. No one needed tequila at this point (it hasn't passed my lips since!). But we drank it anyway. It would have been rude not to. Next thing we knew, we were all spewing over the side railings of the bar and into the Yarra, as the good people of Melbourne went about their day. Not ideal.

We were due to fly to the Gold Coast that night, but there was a strike at the airport so our departure was delayed. And, yes, you guessed right, despite our tequila setback, we went back to P.J. O'Brien's for the evening. Those were the days.

Apart from the partying, the series was really special. My dad had flown out to watch, as I didn't know if I'd get the chance to play for my country again. As it turned out, I played in two more series after that. But, at the time, I played as if I would never have the opportunity again. Having Daddy there to see me wear the jersey and sing the anthem is something I'll never forget.

We won the second match by 21 points, despite our far from professional preparation. Of all the sporting occasions I've been lucky enough to be a part of, International Rules is close to the top of my list of favourites. The series was eventually cancelled because it was 'bringing back the biff' to a level that the GAA didn't want to see. When the series was in Australia, it was morning time in Ireland and Irish schoolkids would get time off to watch it. Sometimes, they'd end up watching more brawling than footy, and no one wanted that.

There was also a belief that the International Series promoted the recruitment of Irish players to the AFL and showed fans that players like me existed, players who could leave Ireland and make the transition quickly. This was not a career path that the GAA wanted to advertise to its talented players.

For all of those reasons, the series was culled. The last one took place in 2017 and, at the time of writing, no further series are scheduled. This is a real shame, as in indigenous codes like Gaelic football and AFL it's the only opportunity we have to represent our countries. The end of the series has meant the end of that.

I'd love to see it return and, if it does, it would be great to see a women's series too. I've been really proud to see the number of Irish women who've made an impact in the AFLW. Why not bring it back and make it a double series? Our shared history and connection mean too much to just let it die.

With the close of the 2011 International Rules Series, my first year of playing AFL was done and dusted, ending on a massive high. But there were tough times ahead at the Blues.

2012 was a tumultuous year for Carlton. It's fair to say they've had a few of those years of late. Sorry, Blues fans (I'm hoping some of you are reading this).

In pre-season, we were optimistic about our prospects and openly talking about a top-four finish. While the team was optimistic, I was not. I was still shy about talking about my ambition to lock down a regular place in the side.

In one pre-season meeting, we were put into groups to set goals. Each group had to pick the best team for the year. I was asked if I thought I would play every game. Of course, I wanted that and thought I should be part of the starting lineup, but for me to argue that meant that I would have to suggest someone to be dropped. I was asked If I thought I could displace Jordan Russell from the starting lineup. Jordan was suggested as he was a similar style player to me, and a very good one at that. I had too much respect for Jordan to sit there and say I deserved his spot after only 11 games. We all picked him as a certain starter, and I agreed, although I felt uneasy about how that could be interpreted by the coaching group. I was just being respectful, but would they see it as a sign that I lacked confidence?

I ended up playing 19 games that year, while Jordan played seven.

It's hard to believe now, but after wins in our first three games, including a 10-goal demolition of Collingwood, we were one of the Premiership favourites. On a personal level, the win over Collingwood was really special, as my sister Naomi was there to see it. She was travelling around Australia and made sure she fit in a match at the G. She picked a good one.

She had helped me so much in my early days and was always on the other end of the phone if I had an issue. Having her there, as we cemented Premiership favouritism, made it twice as good.

However, as Blues fans will be painfully aware, a reality check was imminent. In round four, we played Essendon. They brutalised us for four quarters. I remember standing there thinking, *Where is this coming from?* They were incredibly physical; they had just gone to a new level. I didn't think about it much at the time, I was just shocked at our inability to compete with them.

For those reading in Ireland who may not be aware, an investigation into Essendon's supplements programme during that season resulted in the club being banned from the 2013 finals series and the coach James Hird being suspended. In 2016, 34 players were suspended for two years, which affected 17 players still active in the competition. It came close to destroying the club. I don't mention this to reopen old wounds for Bombers fans, as the topic has been done to death; it is only documented here for context.

Back to the Blues and, after six rounds, we were sitting pretty at second on the ladder. Then, we lost six of our next seven matches – going from 5–1 (wins–losses) to 6–7 – and found ourselves tenth on the ladder (for Irish readers, the ladder refers to the table, as we would call it). That's where we would eventually finish, missing out on the finals for the first time since 2008.

That season also marked the start of my back issues. I had been tolerating a sore back for a while and in the build-up to our round-16 game against North Melbourne, it had deteriorated a bit. The soreness was just a result of wear and tear. There's rarely a time when you're not managing some sort of niggle during your career, and this was no different. But I wasn't sure if I was going to be ready to play. They decided to put me through a pre-game fitness test to make sure I was up to the rigours of AFL footy.

It was during that fitness test that I bent down to pick up the ball and my whole back spasmed. I'd already taken everything I could from a pain relief point of view so, when this happened, there was nowhere to go. I did my best to recover but I couldn't move. I was a late withdrawal and when we went back into the sheds I popped my head into the coaches' room to let Ratts know. He was great about it. He immediately told me not to worry and to just take it easy and recover.

After my late withdrawal, I went for scans and ended up having my first epidural. Now for anyone reading who thinks that epidurals are just for having babies, let me tell you, they're even more effective for footballers with back issues. When I say epidurals are effective, they are … after a few days. In my experience, the immediate aftermath isn't pleasant. You kind of get worse before you get better – really stiff and sore, and you can't drive. But then you get the relief you crave and you can slowly start the process of a full return to training.

While my back issue was a setback, there was one silver lining. I had to take two matches off, but when I was available for selection again I went straight back into the senior team for our round-18 match against Richmond. We won by four points, and I remember being told what a good sign it was to get straight back in without a trip to the VFL. At the time, I was still searching for confidence and confirmation I had cemented my spot, and this was the confidence boost that I needed.

The end of the season was drama-filled. Having talked

about a top-four spot in the pre-season, we were in danger of missing out on finals altogether. Ratts, who had been given a two-year contract renewal at the end of the 2011 season, was under pressure.

If you're reading this in Ireland, it's time for an explainer on how the AFL media works. When sports reporters smell a coach's blood, there's a violent frenzy that usually ends with the coach's head on a stick. It is not like at home, where you might find out that a coach has left their county on the *Six One News*. Here, they wait for the coach in the car park of the club, and they've even been known to go to their houses, if they're really hogging headlines. The same can go for players. I'm pleased to say I haven't done anything to warrant a house visit, yet.

Our mid-season capitulation meant there was intense speculation over whether Ratts would be sacked, and so the typical media circus ensued. I was still new to all of this, so it was my first true experience of regular media stakeouts in the car park. It wouldn't be my last experience of that – or of a coach being sacked at Carlton. (Apologies again, Blues fans. If you're still reading, you may want to skip to Chapter 7 to avoid any further triggers. Or perhaps you'll find it all therapeutic – I have.)

Despite the off-field saga, we were still in finals contention until the penultimate round of the home-and-away season. The match that put us out of the finals equation, mathematically, was a thrashing by the Gold Coast Suns.

Not that you'd need to be a mathematician to work out how bad we were that day.

One of the most unfortunate stats from that encounter was the fact my best friend, Levi, kicked 0.5 (that's zero goals and five points). Now I know what you're thinking and, yes, we even said it to him. Levi, the guy that helped me get my debut by 'borrowing' my car, got Ratts sacked. That was the joke in the locker room at the time.

If you're reading this in Ireland and thinking five points, especially if they were scored from play, is a good contribution, I'll explain that in Australian Rules you earn a point for a behind. That's when you miss the big sticks for six points (a goal) and, instead, get a consolation point for being inside one of the two outside posts. Some might say it's a point for a wide, but it's not actually wide unless you miss all of them, and then it's called 'out on the full'. You of course get zero points for that. Levi's job was to get six-pointers, so 0.5 wasn't ideal.

Very soon after, we learned there were mitigating factors to his performance. He had copped a knee in the side in a collision but kept playing. After the match he wasn't feeling great.

'I'm pissing blood,' he told me in the dressing rooms after.

'That's not normal,' I said. 'You really need to go and see the doctor, man.'

He did. It turned out that Levi, who we were jokingly

saying was getting Ratts sacked, had suffered kidney damage. He ended up being stretchered out of the changing room to be transported straight to a Gold Coast hospital. He couldn't even fly home with us.

Completely separate, and unrelated to Levi's 0.5 and his kidney damage, Brett's contract was cut short by a year. His last game as coach was the last round of the 2012 season – a dead rubber against the St Kilda Saints. I wasn't playing as they were resting me in case I exacerbated my back issues. Other than a farewell for Ratts, the outcome didn't really mean anything. We lost by 15 points. St Kilda missed out on playing the finals too, finishing in ninth spot, just one place above us.

You might be surprised to hear this, but it made for quite a pleasant week. Ratts had time to say his goodbyes. His exit was classy – he even praised the club for making the decision. It couldn't have been easy for him, as he would already have been aware that the club was courting his replacement, Mick Malthouse.

I'll admit that when he was sacked, part of me was relieved. At this point, I still hadn't fully warmed to the idea that he liked me and that my career was best served under his tutelage. I still had this impression he didn't like Irish players. I was 23 and trying to become an established player, and I had hung on to that idea for far too long. Despite how well he had treated me when I broke into the senior team, I still felt like a change could serve my career well. I'm embarrassed to say that now, but it's how I felt at the time.

While I was excited about having a new coach, I was a little apprehensive about Mick Malthouse's arrival. As one of the most high-profile figures in the game, I didn't know how he'd feel about me, an Irish player and a newer member of the team. I expected him to come in and train us military style, to be old school and put the fear of God into us.

I watched him on TV a lot in the lead-up to his first visit to the club, but it was a whole other experience to see him in real life for the first time. When he walked into the club with that Carlton polo top on, he just had an aura about him. I was wary of him at first, but that wariness was completely misplaced. It turned out that he loved a special project, and he loved players who have had to face adversity to get to where they are. Irish players were the perfect fit for him.

He also loved a war analogy and showing the team war films was part of his repertoire. Contrary to what I expected, he didn't smash us at training – at least not in a completely old-school way. While pre-season was tough and there was a lot of running, he didn't want us smashing each other. He didn't want an injury toll before the season started, and I was thankful for that.

As always, at the end of 2012, I went home and played for my club in Portlaoise. I wasn't sure if Mick would be up for this and decided that, if he wasn't, I'd approach it the same way I did with Ratts. In my first off-season, I did the right thing and asked for permission. When Ratts said 'absolutely not', I did what any good clubman would do. I played anyway. After that, I stopped asking for permission so I wouldn't be doing the wrong thing by not following orders. That was my thought process, and I'm standing by it!

At Carlton, we would have time off after our last game of the season (the end of August if we didn't make finals) until the end of October. We would be back in full training at the beginning of November, which was annoying, as I always missed the Melbourne Cup. The famous horse race is run on the first Tuesday of November every year. Unfortunately, on that day, we would usually be in the midst of hellish pre-season training.

When visiting home, I felt like I owed it to Portlaoise to play for them. After all, if it wasn't for them, I wouldn't be playing professional sport. In my view, it was the very least I could do. I understood the club's concerns that I could get injured, and they were right.

It's fair to say their concerns were fully validated when one off-season I decided to play, despite already being injured. I was on crutches when I arrived in Ireland. I'd had my knee cleaned out in a procedure called an arthroscopy. Nothing serious but, clearly, having been given crutches for my recovery, the recommendation would have been that the last thing I should do was play Gaelic football.

I played anyway. Yes, you read that right. Ridiculous, I know.

I remember being concerned that this particular time they would find out. It's not exactly inconspicuous when an Aussie Rules player leaves his crutches on the bench to play club football.

When I got back, our assistant coach John 'Barks' Barker asked me how my off-season had been. A harmless enough question, but he fairly quickly steered the conversation towards whether or not I'd played any football. I had a sneaking suspicion he knew I had played, so I decided to self-report. 'I just went on for a few minutes and I didn't do much,' I said.

As if that made it okay.

He looked at me sharply, with a mixture of incredulity and suspicion.

Then, he gave me a wry grin and carried on with his day. I never heard about it again. He must have weighed it up and deemed it unworthy of punishment. Barks was good like that, and he knew how much the club meant to me. I was grateful for that.

The full story was that I had arrived in Ireland on crutches, but I had stopped having to use them just before the game. That crutch-using stint of my life was over so, technically, I was in prime physical condition.

The full story about the match was that I had played the whole thing. I'm pretty sure John didn't believe my version of events, but I had passed my medical on return, so he let bygones be bygones.

Irish AFL players at other clubs didn't find it so easy to contribute to their home clubs in the off-season – like Conor Nash, for example. Hawthorn had told him not to play when he went home, and he employed the same tactic of agreeing not to, but doing it anyway. On Conor's return to Australia, his coach, Alastair Clarkson, called Conor into his office and made it clear that due to a Facebook post he was well aware of Conor's Gaelic football exploits. He got a talking to.

What I concluded from this was that the Hawks had contacts keeping an eye on their players' off-season adventures, but that clearly Carlton didn't.

Now that Mick Malthouse was taking over, who knew what the regime would be during the season or after it?

I was lucky – Mick warmed to me straightaway.

The 2013 season was a relatively successful one for me, and for Mick Malthouse. For the first time, I played every match. I was one of five players at the club to do that – a group that included a legend of the club, Kade Simpson. And we finished in the top eight … just about. We actually finished ninth, but Essendon was banned from the finals series after an investigation into their supplement programme, so we moved from ninth to eighth.

Our last home-and-away match of the season was a thriller against the Port Adelaide. We were trailing by a whopping 39 points, but a fourth-quarter blitz saw us finish winners, by a solitary point. We kicked four goals in the first eight minutes of the final quarter, and we could feel it was on. The match was in Adelaide and you could sense their supporters were stunned. By the way, there is nothing better than silencing an Adelaide crowd. I mean that in the most respectful way as the match atmosphere is always epic. The Power's Matthew Broadbent had the chance to kick the winner with a 50-metre set shot attempt, with just 27 seconds to go. His kick hit the post, leaving Port with a one-point deficit. We'd hung on, for dear life.

That win, because of the location, the nature of the comeback and what it meant for the club, was one of the most exhilarating of my career. Our skipper, Marc Murphy, kicked three goals and Bryce Gibbs was a standout with 26 possessions. Andrew Walker was instrumental, while Eddie Betts, Chris Yarran and Jeff Garlett kicked two goals each. We were high on confidence going into our elimination final with Richmond.

That day against Richmond, Dusty Martin showed flashes of the brilliance that would eventually see him become a three-time Norm Smith medallist and a triple Premiership player. He kicked a cracking goal in the second quarter and the Tigers looked fired up, but it turned out to be Carlton's day.

Chris Judd had stepped down as captain at the beginning of the year and Marc Murphy had taken over but, as always,

Chris was a leader on the field, kicking one of the goals that sealed our semi-final spot. When Jeff Garlett ran into the goals to kick our final major, the Carlton crowd sent the stadium off the Richter scale and Richmond fans were spewing, which we love. We won by 20 points in the end to secure a match with the Sydney Swans. Because of our underdog status, this win meant a lot to the group.

But that was where our good run ended. After three significant wins in a row, maybe we ran out of steam, maybe we had nothing left in the tank. We trailed by 22 points at half-time against the Swans, but we lost it altogether in the third quarter. We failed to kick a single point while the Swans booted five goals. We ended up losing to the Swans by 24 points at Sydney Olympic Stadium. It was one of many tussles we had with them.

I think the consensus from early in the season was that we probably weren't going to be a real force come September, and our ceiling that year was just making finals. Given that we made finals, albeit in very unusual circumstances, the season wasn't a complete failure, and the way we finished felt like a good grounding for progression the following year.

At least that was the feeling in the club.

I came seventh in the John Nicholls medal for Best and Fairest, which was massive. I felt like I'd finally 'made it'. Not from a success point of view, but I now knew I had cemented my spot in the team.

One of the big stories of the off-season that year was the

departure of Eddie Betts and the signing of Daisy Thomas.

Losing Eddie from the team was a far bigger loss than anything we'd experienced on the field.

For those reading in Ireland, it's hard to put Eddie's impact, on and off the field, into context. One of the most gifted players to have played Aussie Rules, his whole career was a highlights reel. Famous for his awe-inspiring goals, he's equally well known for being a voice for his people off the field. Far too many times, Eddie has had to speak up against racism aimed at Aboriginal people in Australia.

The thing that really stings, and would hurt supporters most to hear, is that, at the start, Eddie had absolutely no interest in leaving Carlton. I think there was some minor disagreement over contract terms that couldn't be resolved, so off Eddie went to the Crows on a four-year deal. The move ended up being advantageous for Eddie, from the point of view of on-field performances at least.

Daisy was so highly rated at the time, and coaches and list-management teams have to make these decisions constantly – sometimes, they get it wrong. Any team at the time would have loved to have had Daisy at their club, so trying to bring him in made perfect sense, however, the decision to let Eddie go will, with the benefit of hindsight, go down as one of the all-time howlers when it comes to list management. The narrative around his signing was that the teacher's pet was on his way to the club. Daisy had always been a favourite of Mick's at Collingwood. They would handball to each other in the warm up rooms before matches and commentators had picked up that it was part of Mick's pre-match routine. There was pressure on the decision, and on Daisy to perform. He ended up staying a lot longer than Mick did in the end, playing 101 games for the club until retiring at the end of 2019.

At this point, I'm just hoping Blues fans really did skip forward to Chapter 7 as this will be hard to read.

When I describe it as a howler, I acknowledge that hindsight is a wonderful thing. Wouldn't every recruiter be the best in the world if they could look 10 years into the future? Daisy was a highly rated addition to our squad, but Eddie went on to play out the peak years of his career at another club, even making a Grand Final with the Adelaide Crows in 2017. Even Carlton fans would have enjoyed watching him thrive.

Eddie is such a good guy and there was a big knock-on effect in the change room when he left. We didn't just lose Eddie for his prime years, we lost other players because of his departure. Two of our biggest talents left in the years after. Jeff Garlett moved to Melbourne at the end of 2014 and Chris Yarran (Yaz) departed after the 2015 season.

Yaz moved to Richmond, but he never played a senior game there. He has had challenges off the field, but when he was at Carlton, he was the most talented player I've ever shared a field with. He was frighteningly good. Chris Judd (Juddy) has said he's one of the most-talented players he's ever seen. High praise from him after everything he'd achieved and the ilk of players he'd been surrounded by at West Coast. Juddy was right. Yaz was an absolute freak. I've never seen anything like him.

As well as his effect on individual players, Eddie was the glue that kept the change room together. He didn't stick to any one clique and, at that time, the change room was a little bit cliquey.

In my first season at the club, he invited me over to his house for drinks. I remember he pulled me aside that evening and discreetly asked if I wanted to go to a nightclub in town or just stay at his place for a quieter night. I remember thinking I should just do whatever he wanted to do. That's the level of influence that older, successful players in the team can have on younger players, and he always used his influence for good. I really appreciated him checking in with me to make sure I was comfortable.

As well as being incredibly gifted, he's just a great human being. But you don't need me to tell you that. We continue to see that in the way he has conducted himself in the media since he retired and the dignified way he copes with the racism he and his family, and players from his community, have had to endure. He's all class.

When I say the locker rooms were a bit cliquey, I should point out that the big names were never the ones who made them that way. Considering who Chris Judd was, and his stature in the game, he didn't have to talk to any of us kids, but he always did. And when he stepped away from the role of captain and Marc Murphy took over, I noticed the big effort Marc made to mingle with everyone and connect us all – not an easy task because he had a difficult dynamic with Mick Malthouse, so he was dealing with that as well as the cohesion of the group.

Murph was an exceptional leader and probably underrated in that regard. He worked hard to develop himself in all areas on and off the field, as a footballer and as a captain.

Mick, let's just say, was good at creating difficult dynamics. He loved to hand out sprays and, if you couldn't handle them, things would escalate.

Early in 2014, I was the beneficiary of a spray so big that it made headlines. It was round six and the West Coast Eagles were in control at Etihad Stadium. Spoiler alert – a five-goal blitz in the final term saw us steal a three-point win. But not before Mick blitzed me. I was having a howler, and he was keen to let me know. When I approached the bench after a spectacular turnover, caused by me, he was waiting for me on the boundary. To say he was unimpressed would be the biggest understatement in this book.

The footage of him berating me, and of me trying to get away from him, got everyone's attention. It was such a standout spray that I was interviewed about it after.

'What are you talking about, mate?' I said when I was asked about it by the press. 'That's how Mick looks when he's pumping you up,' I joked.

Yes, the footage is available on YouTube, if you're so inclined.

I should point out that the spray worked. When I went back on the field, I won a 50-metre penalty and kicked one of those five goals I mentioned earlier. But I wish there had been a camera on his post-match speech. That's where the gold really was.

'And as for you, Zach,' he smirked at me. 'You were absolutely shit for three quarters, you contributed absolutely nothing to the performance but, in the last quarter, you actually stood up and delivered when we needed you.' These words, or something like it, were delivered in a tone that was as sarcastic and threatening as it was genuinely entertaining. In other words, in a very Mick Malthouse way.

What did I say to that?

'Thanks, I think?' I ventured in an affable tone to avoid any further retribution.

Believe it or not, that's one of my favourite memories of Mick. He's very divisive so not all players would agree with this, but I believe that when he executed a spray, it was very calculated. And I feel like he only did it to players that could take it. Players that would use it as motivation.

With Mick I think there's a common misconception that he would just lose it. In my view, he would plan it. Admittedly, it would take him a while to calm down from a really good bake. He might have got it wrong a few times with players, but I think Mick had the best intentions. He gave me a few sprays over the journey, and I deserved every one of them.

Unfortunately for me, a lot of those sprays occurred during the 2014 season, which was my worst year in AFL.

It was my worst year, but it ended up being Ciarán Sheehan's best, in the AFL at least. He ended up finally signing a contract with Carlton, four years after he was supposed to travel over with me at the end of 2009. He started talking to the Blues again after the International Rules Series in 2013, which we both played in. Ciarán Byrne from Louth had also joined the club. After the departure of the Ó hAilpíns, there were three Irish players at the club again. And that was a massive positive for me, on and off the field.

Sheehan debuted in round 20 that season and played four games. In what was an incredible achievement for him, he was named best first-year player at the Blues. Sadly for him, he only played two more senior games for the club over the next three years before leaving. Persistent injuries sabotaged his career down under, which was so unlucky, because he certainly had the talent to go the distance.

I loved having him back at the club. It was good to see a friendly face and have someone there who I had started my journey with. But I'm not sure how much I was available to him.

I had a lot going on off the field in 2013 and 2014. So much so, I've decided to dedicate a whole chapter to it. That's next.

CHAPTER 5

Wild Ones

I SAID I HAD A LOT GOING ON IN MY PERSONAL life in 2013 and 2014. Before I tell you about that, I need to bring you up to speed on a serendipitous meeting I had at the end of 2011. That's when it all started – like most love stories do – in a dodgy nightclub.

CQ nightclub was, at the time, renowned for being a not-so-classy, footy-player haunt in the city. It was hardly your first port of call when looking for a meaningful relationship but, on this occasion, it delivered.

On this particular night, I was there with my housemate, Levi Casboult, and we were celebrating my twenty-second birthday. Levi and I had been living together for almost a year. There had been many eventful nights in that less-than-12-month period. This one, though, was particularly significant.

At the time, Levi was dating the woman who is now his wife, Hayley, who happened to bring along her friend, Bec.

At one point, Levi and Hayley disappeared. They were doing what young couples tend to do. One minute they would be all over each other, the next they were bickering. We've all been there. They were doing the latter for a while that evening, and Bec maintains that she was 'stuck with me'. The vodka raspberries were flowing, and we were singing and dancing to a song we ended up playing at our wedding – 'Wild Ones' by Flo Rida. Now, when I say we were 'singing and dancing', I can confirm I was doing a lot less of the latter. My version of dancing is standing next to a human who is dancing, while actively encouraging them, and sipping on my drink, perhaps with the odd sway involved. That's the extent of it. Like many athletes, I'm not renowned for my dance moves.

Levi and Hayley eventually returned. They had kissed and made up and Levi, who knew me well at this point, could see I had a certain glint in my eye. Evidently, Bec did too. Understandably smitten by my unkempt appearance and distinct lack of style, she fell head over heels in love with me that night. She tries to deny this, of course, but I've said it so much over the years it has become true because that's how history works.

Anyway, it's important to note that, although we were introduced to each other at CQ, this would blossom into a somewhat serious relationship. Married with two kids qualifies as serious relationship I assume? This is an important distinction, because of the aforementioned reputation of the nightclub at the time – not that there's anything wrong with a nightclub hook-up, I'm just saying. We are happily married now and have two amazing children, who I hope will read this book one day. (Hi Flynn and Rafferty – it definitely wasn't a nightclub hook-up, not that there's anything wrong with that. Talk to me in private.)

So, there I was celebrating my birthday with this girl Bec and looking forward to Christmas in Portlaoise a few weeks later, and I had no idea that, one day, she would be my wife.

About a week later, we met up again before I headed home for my holidays. Levi and Hayley were meeting at an Irish pub, The Quiet Man, and Bec and I tagged along. Our meetings were usually last-minute or informal but, after I returned from my Christmas visit home, we started seeing each other more and more. It was pretty casual to start with. I think we even lost contact for a while. Not for long, mind you, but for a little while. I must admit that I was the one who ended this brief hiatus. I blinked first. I instigated contact again.

That's not what cemented our relationship, though. It was actually my dog, Olly, a husky that you may have seen as a tattoo on my shin, who really brought us together. Bec offered to look after Olly while I went home over the festive season a year later. We still had a pretty casual arrangement almost 12 months on, and I saw straightaway that this was a classic manoeuvre that would force me to contact her again when I returned. She can deny this claim as much as she wants, but who is writing the book?

Now, Olly was a great dog, but he was also a spectacular escape artist. Honestly, he could find a way out of anywhere; there was no lock-up that could hold him. One time, he escaped out of my backyard, got picked up and put in the pound, only to spring himself free by climbing up the iron fence! Even the staff were impressed.

I had mentioned this possibility to Bec – probably – and it wasn't long before she saw it happen for herself. Or didn't see, because he was there one minute and gone the next. While I was at home celebrating Christmas with my family, Bec called me and was inconsolable, bawling her eyes out. In between sobs, she told me she had put posters all over Camberwell but had heard nothing. Olly's collar had my Australian number on it, so she needed me to check my voicemails to see if he had been picked up.

When I eventually managed to log into my Australian voicemail, there was a lovely message from a stranger that just said: 'Hi, just letting you know we've picked up Olly. He's with us now and we had a great day taking him to the beach with our dog. They got on great.'

As poor Bec was crying her eyes out, and I'm up at all hours trying to access my voicemail, Olly was having a day out at the beach!

If Bec was going to cry that much over Olly going missing, that reflected really well on her as a human being, so from that moment on I knew she was the girl for me. When I got back on 8 January, we had the chat and officially became a couple.

A few months later, our relationship went to the next level. Like a rocket. It was a Monday morning in April, and Bec and I had met for dinner the night before. As usual, I left to go into the club early the next day. Bec usually stayed at mine and went straight to work. But when I got home after training, she was still there – sitting on my bed in her pyjamas, her face drained of any colour.

She hadn't gone to work that day, she said.

I was wondering what was going on and probably thinking about dinner.

'I went to the hospital instead,' she said.

That fairly focused my attention.

'I hadn't been feeling well and thought I was pregnant ...'

Gulp.

'I did a test and it showed up negative, but I knew something wasn't right so I went to the hospital to get

checked out. They did all the tests and ... I *am* pregnant.'
And with that she completely broke down in tears.

'This will end up being the best thing that's ever happened,'
I said, wrapping her in a hug. I really meant it too but,
looking back, I reckon I might have been shell-shocked.

I totally understood her reaction. It was completely
unplanned and it was changing Bec's life. I was excited. I
reassured her that everything would be okay. I had good
reason to believe this because my sister Naomi got pregnant
when she was young and while that was obviously a huge
deal at the time, I had seen how things that you fear, but
are inevitable, can become wonderful. Of course, I knew
it wouldn't be easy but, years on, I knew that there was no
way we'd ever regret this happening to us. It could only be
a blessing.

The first time Bec met my parents was on FaceTime, and
she was pregnant. Now, I don't know if it's an Irish thing or
universal, but this is not the textbook ideal start on how you
want your mum and partner to meet. I took some advice
from Naomi, who was delighted of course. She assured me
that there was no time to dally, so we barrelled in.

My parents were in Turkey at the time for my other sister
Hannah's wedding. Mammy's reaction was one for the ages.

'This is Bec,' I said, fairly sheepishly.

'Hello Bec,' says Mammy sweetly.

'And we're, er, pregnant.'

Mammy shot to her feet and bolted off the screen. Daddy

sat tight and congratulated us, saying it was fantastic news. He was so warm and welcoming of Bec. We chatted on, but it was getting a bit awkward that there was no sign of Mammy returning. Eventually, she came back and apologised.

Later I found out that when we said we were pregnant, what Mammy heard was, *Your youngest, your baby boy, is never returning from Australia.* She had got very emotional and didn't want us to see that. I'm very close to my family and, if you ask any Irish person about Irish mammies and their sons, you'll hear that the maternal bond is next level.

Mammy made a decent-enough recovery on FaceTime, reappearing back on screen after an anxious couple of minutes for us, but Bec told me later how incredibly relieved she was when they finally met in person. The hug was so warm and tight that Bec knew everything really was all right. Fast forward to now and my parents couldn't love Bec more; sometimes, I think she has gone past me in their affections.

While we told my parents about our news in that first meeting, I wasn't up for telling Bec's parents the first time they laid eyes on me – mainly because of the timing. We had prearranged to have dinner with them, and then we found out our news just two days before we were all due to meet. We decided to go ahead with it as they were in town from Bendigo, but we thought it best not to talk about the pregnancy yet. Bec would have only been five or six weeks gone at that point.

We arranged to meet Deb and Rob at The Snug, a tiny Irish pub on Sydney Road in Brunswick. Very sadly, the pub is no longer. We became close to the Irish couple who owned it, Michael Lynch and Kim Keenan, as well as their chocolate-brown labrador who was always there sitting on the stairs, keeping an eye on the comings and goings of the customers. His name was Keeno. I'm unsure of the spelling but refuse to acknowledge, as a Liverpool fan, that it could possibly have been spelled 'Keano' (yes, I refuse to, despite the fact I like him a lot as a pundit and he was a legend when he played for Ireland). If you know, you know (if you don't, I should tell you this is a Roy Keane reference).

Anyway, it was a regular haunt for us and it was a real Irish pub, not one of those plastic versions with shamrocks and leprechauns everywhere that no self-respecting Irish person would consider legitimate. It was also conveniently located just up the road from the club. And, yes, I can hear what you're thinking: poor Bec, constantly being dragged to Irish pubs. But she enjoys it, honestly! I mean, she clearly has an Irish fetish of sorts.

Dinner went well, we talked about all the usual things. Bec's family are all staunch Richmond fans, including both her parents. But they were polite about Carlton, and I held out hope that one day, they would at least barrack for me (if not the Blues) when we were playing against their beloved Tigers.

It goes without saying the Guinness was good there,

but I didn't have a pint. I was on my best behaviour. For obvious reasons, Bec wasn't drinking, but this didn't raise any alarms with her parents as she wasn't, and still isn't, a big drinker. Anyway, you could barely fit a drink in because of the food portions. Regardless of your meat of choice, it came with all the trimmings, and they had the best gravy in Melbourne. The traditional brown bread was a massive hit too. Oh, how I miss that place.

Luckily, I also happened to be a hit with Bec's parents. I instantly liked them too. They seemed genuinely happy to meet me, but I couldn't help but think, *Yep, this is great, but I wonder how they'll be when they find out Bec's pregnant.*

Just a few weeks later, we decided it was time to head to Bendigo and break the news. We didn't want it to feel like a big deal, so Bec made the excuse that she had to be there for work. As a brand manager, she often does in-store showings, so it made sense for us to pop over if in the area.

I'll never forget driving up to the house. A bungalow on a double block with an ice bath of a swimming pool out the back. I felt good about it all – surprisingly so. I think I was so excited about becoming a dad that it overtook any worries I had about Bec's parents' reaction to it all.

But things got real when we went inside. We were sitting in the kitchen making small talk and all I could think about was when was Bec going to broach this topic. I was leaving the timing of that to her. It was difficult to focus on pleasantries as I waited.

'We have something to tell you,' she said timidly.

Fuck, here we go, I thought.

I was looking at her dad and trying to assess his reaction to her 'something to tell you' announcement. But before I knew it, Bec just blurted it out.

'I'm pregnant,' she said with a cheeky smile.

After a moment, which felt like forever, Bec's mum smiled and hugged us.

'Ohhhhhh,' she exclaimed, before doing so.

Bec translated this reaction for me later as: 'Ohhhhhh, so you're NOT engaged … you're … PREGNANT!!'

Rob congratulated us too, but his reaction was slightly cooler.

That wasn't too bad, I thought. I mean, I'm sure they were concerned, how could they not be? They had basically met me at a pub a few weeks earlier, and now this. I don't remember much about the rest of the evening; it feels like a blur. Maybe I was more relieved that it was over than I cared to admit.

I only found out a lot later that the morning after our visit, Bec's dad, Rob, had called her for a chat. She was his eldest girl and he had always been very protective of her. Understandably, he was checking in to see if I was fair dinkum about it all. The fact I have used the phrase 'fair dinkum' in the right context to describe this interaction also demonstrates that I deserve the citizenship I qualified for years later. Irish readers will probably know this phrase from *Home and Away*. It is the most Aussie phrase of all time and, although I was not a fan of the soap, I believe Alf Stewart used it a lot.

These days, with my new Aussie citizenship and as a dad of two kids, I often look back and think about how lucky we were to have two such supportive families, right from the start. Yes, it was full-on at the time, but them being okay with it all meant everything to us.

The pregnancy went well, and while I was looking forward to the baby's arrival (we decided not to find out the gender), there were times when I worried about the future. Who doesn't? We moved in together in a house in Heidelberg and started preparing for our new arrival. Things were going well, but our relationship was so new that it was hard to really grasp the huge changes that were afoot.

It was while setting up the baby room that it all started to feel real and suddenly hit me. *This is actually happening*, I thought. *What if things go wrong? What will I do then? I can't leave. I can't move home and leave my kid here in Australia. So I'm stuck here now for good. I can't move unless we all do it together.* I was coming to terms with the reality of that, and it was a fairly big weight.

At the club, I was enjoying my football. This year, 2013, was the year I established myself: I played every game.

When I told Mick that Bec was expecting, he was delighted for me. He's a big family guy and I loved his reaction to it. Despite having a lot going on outside of football, I was excelling on the field, and the coach and I were tight. I hadn't experienced the wrath of Mick Malthouse yet. That would come later.

Our new addition was due in January 2014. But two weeks after the expected date of arrival, there was no sign we were going to be a family of three any time soon, so Bec was booked to go into hospital to be induced.

The night before the booked induction, Bec started having contractions at about 10 p.m. They felt different to the Braxton Hicks (false labour pains) she had experienced before, so I drove her straight to the hospital. When we arrived, they tried to send us home, despite the fact she was due to come back a few hours later. We insisted on staying, luckily, and we soon found out that the baby was very close to arrival. Bec was so far along by the time they realised the labour was underway that she couldn't have any painkillers and was going to have to go completely natural.

While Bec missed out on an epidural during both pregnancies (it wasn't possible for our second child years later, either), I have been administered a total of three during my career. Yes, three epidurals. And Bec didn't even get a Panadol. I joke with her that there's one part of pregnancy that I have more experience of than she does. I'm joking but it's true.

At 6.08 a.m. on 20 January, Bec gave birth to a boy. We named him Flynn. Personally, I love the name Fionn, but if we were going to live in Australia, I figured I'd give him a name that was easier to pronounce and save him a lifetime of correcting people. I'll never forget the moment I met him. I was a blubbering mess, and that took me by surprise.

After spending time with Flynn and Bec, I went outside to call my parents. I was fighting back tears already when Daddy said something I'll never forget.

'Maybe now you'll understand why I call you so much,' he said.

That stunned me. Sometimes, when my parents would call, I wouldn't take it. Not because I didn't love talking to them, but maybe I was tired or we had just lost a game and I didn't want a postmortem or the timing was wrong.

Daddy is a serial offender when it comes to talking about football when I'm not in the mood – especially after losses, which I can't stand. Sometimes, I struggle to process my feelings, never mind verbalise them. I don't like to think I'm a bad loser, but it takes me days (sometimes weeks, sometimes forever!) to get over a bad loss. Oblivious to this, and despite my many warnings, Daddy seems to love nothing more than dissecting matches, even when all I want to do is forget them.

As well, he always calls me at the start of the season to tell me what odds we are to win the Premiership. That falls very clearly into the category of stuff I don't want to know. But I know why he does it, and I love that he loves following my career so much, which shows in the granular detail he is willing to go into.

When Dad said that about calling, the waterworks went into turbocharge. Yes, now a father, I knew exactly why he called me so much. There and then, I resolved to never not take his call again. And I've stuck to that ever since.

That moment, and being shown how to bathe and swaddle a baby, is pretty much all I remember from the hospital. Before you know it, you're out the door and expected to look after a little human (even though you can barely look after yourself). That's it.

I remember thinking at the time, if I was adopting a cat, I'd have to sign some forms or something. But your own baby? No, you just get to take it home. I couldn't believe they just let us leave. They didn't even tell us what to do if he cried.

Not only that, I had to drop Bec home and go straight into the club for training. An hour after bringing home our firstborn, and with no idea what to do, I had to leave them both and go to work. The life of a footballer.

In the days leading up to Flynn's birth, I'd stopped going in to the club. I didn't want to leave Bec at home on her own, in case she went into labour, because Carlton's training facility was 30 minutes or more from where we lived.

The club was fine with my brief sabbatical, but when I spoke to Mick on the phone shortly after Flynn's birth, while he congratulated me, he also asked if I wouldn't mind coming back to training.

I had that conversation with him outside the front door

of the hospital. As conversations with Mick go, this was a very polite, I would say even timid, request. I'm lucky that I always had a great relationship with him. And I also knew it was a fair request, given it was my job after all. As polite as he had been, I was left in no doubt that I needed to get back to training. Before I knew it, I was at the club, and I couldn't believe I had a new son waiting for me when I got home from work that evening.

As any parent of a newborn knows, it's the sleep deprivation that gets you and makes everything so hard. Don't get me wrong, Bec did the lion's share of the work while I was at training, which I appreciated enormously. But as athletes, we obsess over maintaining the perfect preparation to maximise our performance and then, suddenly, your sleep is disrupted and at other times severely diminished, and that is tough to handle. We would later find out that Flynn had silent reflux, which was causing a lot of his sleep issues and meant that he often didn't want to feed – a pretty shitty combination.

The fact that we lived thousands of miles away from my family and my support network made it even worse. And it's not as if Bec's parents lived next door either – they lived 150 km away. As the months wore on, I was finding this aspect of having a new baby progressively tougher to deal with. I hadn't struggled badly with homesickness in my career up until then, but having a newborn and not being close to family brought it all to the forefront. Before then, I'd watched on, kind of bemused, as other Irish players left the AFL because they couldn't handle being so far from loved ones. That had never been an issue for me, because I'd always known I'd head back to Ireland at some point and just wanted to see what I could achieve while the opportunity was here.

One particular night stands out. Flynn wasn't sleeping well and Bec was absolutely wrecked. I got up in the middle of the night to give him a bottle. But he didn't want the bottle. And he wouldn't stop crying. I'll never forget sitting on the couch with him, in the dark, and just feeling so alone, so bad about myself. I was totally in my head.

I think if one other person had been sitting there, just to say everything was going to be okay, that this is the hard part, I would have felt better. But there wasn't, and I didn't. It was as low as I've ever felt.

At that time in my life, no doubt, in the scheme of things, the most special period of my life, nothing felt okay. Ireland felt further away than ever and, even when I could sleep, football wasn't going well at all. Life at Carlton was not good. I was so sleep deprived, so empty, so frustrated. That night it all hit me. Despite my measured build-up to this massive life change, I just wasn't coping. They say problems seem worse in the dark – that definitely rang true for me.

I told you that, throughout 2013, I was never on the end of one of Mick Malthouse's legendary sprays. I had played every game and we were tight. I also told you about a very dramatic, televised episode on the boundary during the 2014 season, that I laughed off in the media the following week. But the truth is, Mick had noticed I was out of form much earlier than that, and he was right.

We were playing an intra-club game at Princes Park. I was depleted emotionally and physically. But it was just an intra-club match. I would feel better when the season proper came around – at least that's what I hoped. I thought I was doing enough for how I felt to slip under the radar.

Mick didn't think so.

'You have one good year and you think that you can come in here and just dance around?' he yelled at me, in front of the entire squad.

Then there was silence. It was a warm summer evening in Melbourne, and I felt like I could hear the tepid breeze blowing over me. The only other audible noise was the heavy breathing of my teammates, who were spent after a high-intensity battle. But even that stopped as they waited to see how far Mick would take this particular 'pep-talk'.

'Is that it? Is that what you think?!'

I was looking him in the eye as he berated me. You would never look away from Mick. As was customary during an episode like this, everyone else was staring at the ground.

After more awkward silence, it was over. I hadn't responded and, luckily, that prompted a de-escalation. It could have gone either way.

But I was gutted. *Mick really likes me and he thinks that I played that badly. Wow. I must have been absolutely shit.*

As if I wasn't feeling bad enough as it was (although Mick wasn't to know that – nobody did). I'd gone from a great season to a period where a good day at training was defined by no one noticing how much I was struggling mentally. A good day was my teammates thinking, 'There's Zach, look at him. He's good value.' Irish readers – good value means 'great craic'.

In reality, I was the opposite of that.

That first spray was a sign of things to come. It felt like everything was turning to shit.

I didn't tell any of my teammates what I was going through or how I was feeling. I just couldn't. My whole life, that's how I've approached things. I've thought a lot about why that is while writing this book. And I've learned a lot about myself in the process. One thing I now know is that I'm much more comfortable writing about this sort of stuff for strangers who will read it in future than I am sitting down one-on-one with someone and talking about it. If you're sitting on your own reading this book, then it's the closest I've ever come to confiding in someone.

It's not that I don't believe in all the self-help and well-being stuff, it's just that, for some reason, I feel that opening up and talking about your feelings and being vulnerable is for other people. It doesn't apply to me.

I'll never forget the build-up to our round-eight match against St Kilda that season, but I'll probably never remember the particulars of the match itself. It was a Monday-evening game at Etihad Stadium, and I was getting ready to head out the door. Bec walked into the living room and I was just standing there crying, with my kit bag at my feet.

It had started out of nowhere. It's not like we'd had a fight or anything. We never fight. I couldn't pinpoint exactly what was wrong. But I was sobbing and I was worried it wasn't going to stop. And I had a match to play.

I knew that if I told Mick I couldn't play, he would have been okay with it. Mick was good like that – he was approachable and understanding. But I've always believed that if you are physically capable of playing a match, then you should be playing. During my career, I've played with gastro, broken ribs, torn cartilage in my knee and other assorted niggles. For me, it's not an option not to play.

With a consoling hug from Bec, I picked up my bag and left.

As was the norm, I didn't tell any of my teammates what had happened. I just went through the motions. Saying you cried your eyes out before a match is hardly part of the manual on peptalks in the locker room before a game. I was just hopeful my teammates wouldn't notice my puffy red eyes.

I managed to play relatively okay, and we won. I looked up the score and it turns out that we won by about five goals that night. Apparently, I managed 14 possessions but the ball might as well have been in some other player's hands for all I can remember.

A few weeks later, we were due to play the Brisbane Lions in round 11. I thought maybe, even though my mind wasn't right, I might have been playing well enough to get away with it. I was just scraping through from week to week, but I felt like, in the build-up to this match, I'd camouflaged my melancholy better than usual and trained relatively well – compared to my 2014 level anyway.

But then I got another stern reality check, this time from assistant coach John Barker. Barks approached me in the hallway of the hotel, near the meeting room, on the day before the match.

He basically told me that if there was more depth in the squad, there's no way I'd be playing. He was slightly more tactful in his approach, and I felt like he was trying to help me, but the message was clear. If my performances kept trending this way, it could all be over. I knew I was lucky that there was no pressure from underneath – I didn't need anyone to tell me that – but hearing those words was tough to take. In all my playing days, from school to professional football, I'd never been dropped, apart from that one occasion in 2010 when I went to the VFL reserves.

We ended up losing to the Lions at the Gabba the following evening. Clearly stirred up by the hallway conversation, I kicked a goal. But despite the pretence to my teammates, that everything was okay on the inside, I was close to walking away from all of it.

I just wanted to go back home to Ireland with Bec and Flynn, to be close to family. I didn't want to play football anymore.

I had also started a worrying post-training habit. Every day, on the way home, I would pull over in a street near my house in Heidelberg to have a cry. I stopped in the same place every day. I would see the turn-off for that street coming and my eyes would automatically well up. It wasn't even particularly secluded, but it was convenient. When cars are flying past, they're not exactly looking for crying footballers parked on the side of the road, so it was fit for purpose.

When I was done, I'd drive home and pretend everything was okay. I never spoke to Bec about it. Instead, I gradually withdrew, avoiding eye contact with her in case she saw the redness of tears departed. Not only did I not confide in her, I didn't really talk at all. I was very short with her, just one-word answers, which I feel really bad about now.

I cried a lot that year. And I didn't tell anyone.

Instead, I dealt with it by withdrawing from everything and everyone I could. And by googling jobs in Ireland. I was trying to find something that would match my salary here that I would enjoy. I soon realised that I would have to take a pay cut if I chose that option. I couldn't do that to Bec or Flynn. Because of the way my dad approached life – doing a job he didn't love so he could give us a better future – I knew I had to do that too. I decided that even if I didn't like football anymore, I had to keep doing it. Keeping my family financially secure had to be the priority.

I look back on that time and I know that it wasn't that I didn't like football. I just didn't like anything. But, as usual, my path forward was clear: I just had to shut the fuck up and get on with it.

If you're having a tough period in life yourself and wondering if just pushing through is the right way to go about it, let me assure you, it isn't. I still don't know why I didn't ask for help or get support. On one occasion, Lachie Henderson, my team-mate and friend, gave me the number of a psychologist. I had told him I wasn't feeling great, but I hadn't gone into detail, despite the fact we were close.

After he gave me that phone number, I went through the same pattern over and over. I would look at the number and promise myself that I'd call and make an appointment. But then I would temporarily snap out of my funk and put it on the backburner again. I would spend this time convincing myself I didn't need it. Not long after, I would come close to reaching out again … and rinse and repeat.

I never did call, and I wish I had; even if it wasn't for me, it would have made things much easier for Bec.

Actually, it was only when I sat down to write this book that it struck me how deep I suppressed those feelings back then, how I bottled it all up. Taking the lid off, because I had to if I was going to write this book, has really helped me to process it all.

When I talk to Bec now about this period, it's obvious she felt similar. She remembers in greater detail the hardship of the daily routine with a newborn, while I only remember the feelings I had that year – maybe because she had to keep the house and family ticking over, and I was focused on trying to rescue my faltering career. Either way, I'm glad she saw fit to put up with me over that period, because lord knows it wasn't easy.

One thing I have learned is that we are all in the same boat in life. Sometimes, you are on the deck of the cruise ship and, sometimes, you are hanging on to the life raft. But we all have our own worries, our own struggles. It's helped me to think of it like that.

I'm no poet but I do love poetry. In one of my favourite poems, 'Good Timber', Douglas Malloch writes: 'The stronger wind, the stronger trees.' I felt like I was facing into the biggest headwind of my life. I went from a year I was really proud of in 2013, to barely scraping through the 2014 season.

Carlton finished thirteenth on the ladder that year. At the club, things were about to get worse – the next season would test whether or not I was good timber.

CHAPTER 6

No Longer Feeling Blue

I'M NOT SURE WHEN THINGS GOT BETTER. ALL I know is that, sometime after Flynn's first birthday, we emerged from the new-parent haze and life felt more normal. The fact that I don't remember when exactly that happened is something a lot of parents will relate to. You just kind of survive the first year and celebrate making it to that milestone birthday.

I was loving footy again and looking forward to the season starting.

Just over a week out from our traditional round-one opener against Richmond, Shane O'Sullivan, who was our football administration manager, came out onto the field during training and handed me a phone. It's never good when that happens.

Training doesn't stop for good news. Training only stops for really bad news.

I took the phone from Shane – it was Bec. 'You need to call your parents straightaway, your granny isn't well.'

I ran inside to a back hallway behind our changing rooms and called my parents. They put me on the phone to Granny. She couldn't speak but I could hear her trying to.

She was dying.

I spoke to her for long enough to tell her I loved her. I was on the verge of tears for most of the conversation – if you could call it that – forcing words out through quivering lips. I felt sick to my stomach. Here I was on a football field, on the other side of the world, saying goodbye to the granny who had brought me Coco Pops in warm milk, who had funded my sticker book collections for years and who never had an issue admitting I was her favourite. The best I could offer in return was a five-minute phone call to her on her deathbed. Fuck sake.

Memories were flooding into my mind. She was leaving us and I couldn't be there.

When I hung up, I remember thinking how weird it was that everything looked the same at Princes Park. Training continued. The sky was still blue – but to me it had a grey hue. My world was changing.

I went straight to Mick and told him what was happening. He told me I could go home to Bec. Mick was always good like that. He was family first at all times and I appreciated it.

What did I do next? Take him up on the offer? No. I went to the weights room and asked our weights coach if I could get my lift done early, before everyone else came off the track. This wasn't the first time, and it wouldn't be the last, that I buried my feelings and went on with business as usual. I was continuing a trend, but I didn't know it back then.

Just shut the fuck up and get on with it, Zach. No one is coming to save you.

I was lifting weights when I found out she had died. It was an hour or so later. Yet again, I learned the heartbreak of being thousands of miles away from family when bad news broke – when they needed me most.

That day was horrendous. But then I did what a lot of people do when they live away from home. I forced myself to block it out. I couldn't make it back for the funeral, so I moved on and tried not to think about it.

Everything looked the same at the club when I returned the next day. My teammates offered their condolences; everyone was lovely. For all I knew, in the way my day-to-day existence continued, Granny could still be alive. I thought it was best to keep it that way in my brain, at least until I had to go home and face it.

What I know now is that I should have gone home to be

with my family. I should have told the club I was leaving, and that was that. I felt like I couldn't do that because the season was about to start and so, instead, I just got on with it. Like I always did.

And there was plenty to distract me at the club. Another turbulent year was brewing.

We had finished thirteenth on the ladder in 2014, and tension was high.

We lost the first three matches of the 2015 season and the spotlight was firmly on Mick's future. We had a short reprieve in round four, beating St Kilda by 40 points.

But in round five, things escalated. It was a major milestone match for Mick. He became the longest-serving coach in the history of the AFL – having coached 715 matches, surpassing Jock McHale's 714.

The only problem was, we didn't exactly mark the occasion in the way Mick would have liked. We got smacked by his former side, Collingwood, to the tune of 75 points.

The guard of honour for Mick at the end of the match is etched into my memory for all the wrong reasons. Players from both sides lined up next to the race (for the benefit of Irish readers – that's the exit from the field down a tunnel to the change rooms) to pay tribute to him. Mick was walking off, waving to the crowd and trying to acknowledge the moment. But there was one issue with that. As much as Mick wanted to soak it up and show the crowd appreciation, he wanted to start punishing us more. He was seething.

As he walked off the field, he was laser-focused on us and giving us boys … a death stare. I mean, if looks could kill, a Mick Malthouse look wouldn't just murder you, it would organise a wake and bury you too. Mick cared about letting us know how horrendous our lives were going to be until the next match much more than he cared about his milestone.

I was surprised but relieved we didn't have a meeting straight after the game. Post guard-of-honour death stare, it would not have been pleasant. Later that night, we received an ominous text message: 'St Kilda Beach. 6 a.m. Recovery.'

It was succinct, but I knew the reality of this message would be long drawn out and not very enjoyable. My instinct was correct. When we got there, it was on. And not in a good way.

We had a tackling coach at the time, John Donehue, or 'JD' as we called him. JD had also been summoned to St Kilda and his appearance did not bode well for us. Mick wasn't there, just Robert Wiley, who was his director of coaching and development at the time. This session, however, had nothing to do with development. We immediately knew it was a punishment session.

There we were, on the sand, in the cold, sumo wrestling and doing commando rolls. It was hell. We were already sore from the match and now we had to wrestle one on one. You're in shorts, topless, so there's nothing to grab on to. You get my drift.

Then, they put us into two groups and we were told to run at each other. There was a line in the middle and you had to knock another guy over the line. Whoever stayed upright, stayed in. After one or two of those, we were wrecked. If you won more than three of those, good luck to you.

I can't remember how long all of this went on for, but it felt like forever. This was much worse than the cold-water swims we had done as punishment when Brett Ratten was at the club. On one occasion, Mitch Robinson had turned up late to a meeting, or maybe missed it altogether, and his punishment was for all of his teammates, not him, to go and jump off St Kilda Pier and swim back to shore – at 6 a.m., in winter, while he watched on. That was a nasty one.

Anyway, this wrestling punishment was making me yearn for those cold-water swims. And that's saying something.

Now, you would think when guys are forced to wrestle, things might get feisty. But, no, not at all. On this morning, in the wake of another depressing loss, we were just trying to make it through. No one was trying to be a hero. We were just trying to get it over with and get the fuck out of there.

When I got back to the car, part of me couldn't believe that being a professional footballer had resulted in mornings like this. We were also forced to go into the club to do a 'normal recovery'.

Now, I've never been into the politics of how a club works or taken any notice of off-field drama, but the circus around Mick and the talk about his future was hard to avoid. Especially when parking your car.

As I explained earlier, when there is any sort of drama at the club, the car park is where the journalists wait – with cameras and mics on – hoping to get a comment from one of the star players. The star players will sometimes stop for a chat and regurgitate the same few lines about how happy they are with the coach and how he has their full support. In case you're wondering, back then I was not a star player, so I was rarely hassled. I could park my Hyundai i45 in peace.

I loved that car. It was the first new car I had ever bought. It was expensive, but I got a discount as they sponsored us, and the new-car smell was free. It was silver with a black roof, and every time I looked at it I reminded myself how lucky I was to have moved on from the perpetually overheated Honda Civic.

Meanwhile, stars like Chris Judd could not park their car so easily. Back then, Juddy would have been driving a top of the range Hyundai and completing his reverse park in the certain knowledge that he was about to have a mic shoved in his face. When that happened, he was always classy, rolling out those predictable lines better than anyone.

Not only was Juddy great in front of the cameras, and willing to take a hit in the car park for the team, he was also brilliant for morale behind the scenes. As you can imagine, things felt pretty sour at the club, but Juddy always had the ability to make us laugh.

The man is multitalented but here's one you might not have heard of – he can rap. Yep, you read that right. His party piece was to write random words on a white board at the club and then get up and rap a song with lyrics using those words. He was fantastic, and we would roar laughing. Not because it was bad or cringeworthy (I'm thinking of Kendall Roy from *Succession* here) – it was really good. I believe his rap name was the 'Vanilla Gorilla'.

Juddy is talented like that. He could make fun out of nothing and he knew when to do it to lift everyone's spirits. If we were doing a tough weights session, he would bounce around the gym, getting in players' faces, while comically shouting, 'This is where we live; we live in the house of pain.'

As well as having an epic sense of humour, as is more well known, Juddy is extremely intelligent and a great speaker too. But what I admired about him most was that he gave every player on the team his time, regardless of the player's seniority and influence or their lack thereof. He's been really successful in business since leaving football and has always been generous with his time when it comes to helping out former teammates – including me.

While Juddy made sure we always looked on the bright side, Mick remained how he had always been. Which meant he was angry some of the time, but mostly he was fine. As I've said, I always had a great relationship with Mick, but he was polarising. At this point, it was pretty obvious that some of the players couldn't stand him. Marc Murphy, our captain at the time, has since admitted he didn't see eye to eye with Mick over this period.

From what I witnessed, Mick had the capacity to fall out with a player and when he did, that was the end of their relationship – or at least that's how it felt. When he had decided your papers were stamped, there was no way back. By the end of Mick's time, I think it's fair to say that Marc Murphy hated him. And that, as you can imagine, made for a weird dynamic. I had the feeling Mick never wanted Murph to be captain in the first place, but that's pure speculation on my part. If it was true, I didn't understand it, because I thought Murph was an excellent captain.

Another factor that made for less than successful on-field outcomes was the gap between players in the change room. There was a big difference between Carlton's top players and their 'bottom' players – financially and ability-wise.

At Carlton, there were some really high rollers on big money, who were earning significantly more than the younger players. If you're on a team like that, it's realistic to say that self-interest, rather than team interest, is generally higher. Carlton had a few of the game's highest-paid players but were languishing at the bottom of the ladder.

It was different at clubs like Hawthorn and Geelong, where their top players were earning less than they could justifiably demand elsewhere, so that money would be more evenly spread, and the team as a whole would be stronger. Carlton was taking a financial approach to winning Premierships: buying individual talent, rather than focusing on building a strong, overall team.

One by-product of this approach was that in the Blues locker room the higher-profile players didn't hang out with the younger no-names. I mean, those younger players couldn't even afford dinner at the restaurants the high rollers were going to.

If you were one of the younger players at Carlton, you were desperately trying to stand out and show what you were capable of, so you could become established. If you were an older, highly paid player, of course you want to win but, if you didn't, you were still walking away with heavy pockets. I don't think that's a good dynamic to have in a group.

It felt like there wasn't a middle tier of guys trying to push up the standard. There were just guys who were trying to get a gig or guys who were trying to earn money. None of which manifested itself in a good team performance. It was a cocktail for loser-ish behaviour.

I hate to admit this, but towards the end under Mick, losing became an expectation. And we weren't just losing, we were getting pummelled. Honourable losses were welcomed as a relief because at least you felt you weren't going to be publicly decimated.

That win against St Kilda was our last victory under Mick. The four losses in a row, which had started with this 715th match, ended up being the end of the road for him and the Blues.

As I said, he was at war with the club publicly and it all ended in a very public way.

The suits had indicated that they would consider his future after the bye round. Mick did an interview and was openly critical of the administration and the board. A couple of days after the broadcast, he got what we all felt he must have wanted. He was sacked. It had felt like he was asking for it for a while.

Mick had only lasted eight rounds of the 2015 season.

As always, Juddy was swamped by press in the car park. He said, 'The main emotion is one of sadness for Mick because he's a wonderful coach and has really been put through the wringer throughout this whole process.' Juddy – classy as always.

Mick left the club on the Tuesday before our round-nine, Friday-night match against the Sydney Swans. In the AFL, matches are played across three days of the weekend – Friday to Sunday – however, in recent times, Thursday nights have also become a popular fixture. Throughout, one thing has remained the same: Friday night is the blockbuster match.

When the AFL plans the year, the best teams with the biggest followings and prospects get scheduled to play under Friday-night lights. And, no, the AFL would not have been planning for a losing Carlton side, with a new caretaker coach, to occupy that spot, but here we were, again.

The club promoted assistant coach John Barker to interim senior coach while they started the search for a permanent replacement. As a playing group, we were aware that Barks was applying for the role full-time. Because of that, his style had to change a bit. Barks had always been the 'good cop' to the senior coaches' (Ratten and Malthouse) 'bad cop' routine. He would insert some humour into team meetings and try to make you feel better if you had been on the end of a big spray. As you can imagine, this was invaluable when Mick had been in charge.

He had a segment in meetings where he would play a video of a player messing up so we could laugh at it. It was always good-natured and it helped break the ice. After he took over as interim, he had to step back from that light-hearted stuff. He delegated that meeting task to Daisy Thomas. Barks was still great one-on-one with players and maintained that lighter side, but at team meetings he became more serious.

It was a relief when he took over. It had been so tense for so long at the end of Mick's tenure. Mick's departure meant the cameras left the car park, and that made for a much more pleasant arrival to training.

It was freeing mentally too, and it was great on the field, as we had the freedom to play an exciting style of football. Barks had a different game style.

He replaced Mick's territory style and kick-chase method with a 'paint the fence' approach. To him, this meant he wanted us all to spread out, right to the boundary, and take on the game. He wanted us to attack and attempt to spread the opposition, so we could kick our way through them.

Initially, we played really well under the new regime, as teams often do when a new coach comes in. We lost to the Sydney Swans by 60 points three days into his tenure, which wasn't great obviously, but the following week was a major improvement – we fell short against the Adelaide Crows by just nine points.

Then, lo and behold, we won not one but two matches in a row, beating Port Adelaide and the Gold Coast Suns. Having become accustomed to losing, this was a great feeling.

Unfortunately for Barks, that was as good as it got. We only won one match out of our remaining 10. His three wins out of 14 games senior-coaching record didn't exactly help his chances of securing the gig long term.

Aside from his record, I don't think he ever really had a chance, and I think we all knew that. We also knew why. At the time, Hawthorn assistant coaches were all the rage. Everyone wanted an Alastair Clarkson understudy. Damien

Hardwick had left Hawthorn to take the senior role at Richmond (although he was yet to win the first of his three Premierships) and Luke Beveridge was at the Western Bulldogs (he would lead them to the 2016 Premiership).

The Clarko disciples were hot on the market, and Carlton decided they needed one to turn it all around. On 24 August 2015, Brendon Bolton, who was an assistant to Clarko at Hawthorn, was announced as our new senior coach.

It was awkward for Barks, who had to coach out the season. I felt for him.

Speaking of awkward, my first official meeting with Brendon Bolton was exactly that. We were briefly introduced at the awards for Best and Fairest Player of the Year, but it wasn't until he arrived at the club for pre-season that we had our first one-on-one.

I was feeling pretty good after the Best and Fairest. I had just been named on the AFL Coaches Association All-Australian team as the best 'small defender', and I'd turned around my form from my dismal showing in 2014 to the extent I came third in the John Nicholls medal – finishing just four votes behind Patrick Cripps, and three behind the skipper, Marc Murphy.

We were brought into Brendon Bolton's office to meet him individually, and Shane O'Sullivan, who had been at the club for decades, was also there. Shane had seen it all at this point, God love him.

'What helps you to play well, to be at your best?' Brendon enquired.

'I perform well when I'm given specific roles. I can execute them really well – I just need clarity on my role,' I said.

Back then, I was given jobs on some of the opposition's best players. Richmond's Dusty Martin and Adelaide Crows' Patrick Dangerfield were some of the players I was instructed to contain. I often lined up on the likes of Stephen Milne, who was a nightmare to defend against, Cyril Rioli and even Eddie Betts, after he moved to Adelaide.

The thing about Eddie was he could be having a really quiet game and you could feel like you were doing really well on him. But then, out of nowhere, he would snap two goals from the pocket, on his wrong foot, and it was like, *Really?! What the fuck just happened? He's done nothing for an hour and 40 minutes and then in a hectic blitz, he's just done that to me.*

Despite those experiences, I loved being given a specific job. It's funny when I look back on that conversation, as I've changed so much as a player. I enjoy the opposite now.

'As a club, what do we need to do to get better?' he continued.

'I'm not sure. But what I do know is that this place has been pretty fucking miserable to come to work at for a while. It would be nice if blokes enjoyed coming to work again.'

He looked like he was taking this on board. Then his

line of questioning escalated. 'Would you be ready to play a game this weekend? Where is your fitness at?'

I didn't know what to say. The truth was, no, of course I wasn't ready to play. It was the off-season. We'd just come back from time off. We were starting pre-season, and pre-season is what makes you ready. But you never know what a new coach wants to hear from you. I hedged my bets.

'I'm as fit as I've been at this time of year and I've completed every session of the off-season programme, but, no, I'm not ready to play.' I was confident that this was a good response.

'What do you mean you're not ready to play?' he replied.

Gulp. Hedging my bets had not worked. I had to recover quickly. The last thing I needed was to get off on the wrong foot with the new coach.

'Well, it's the off-season and it's been a tough year, with everything that happened, and I took time to go away and unwind,' I said.

What I wanted to say was, *If you wouldn't mind going and getting fucked that'd be great thanks, champion.*

When I look back on this first chat, I know that, effectively, this was the beginning of the end for me and Bolts, and me and the Blues. And all before we'd started pre-season.

But in the beginning, I was desperate to make it work. When you're working on a relationship of any kind, and I've never had to work so hard on a relationship as I did with

My home town of Portlaoise is known for two things: football and a prison. That prison was where my dad worked, and here you can see him in the uniform he wore every workday through my childhood. That job gave Mammy a few scares over the years, but it also left us with some excellent stories. I feel incredibly lucky to have been able to do a job I love so much after seeing what my father put up with.

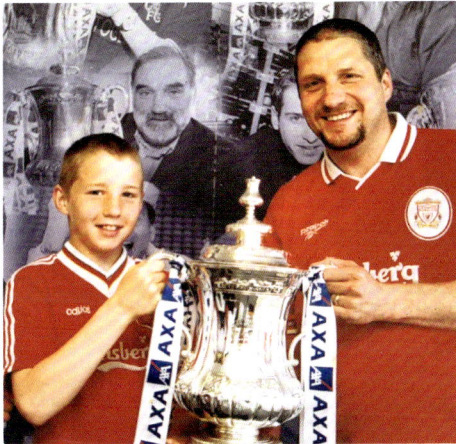

As a kid I was more interested in soccer than Gaelic football. Here's me and the old man holding what we were told was the real FA Cup trophy on tour in Portlaoise. I highly suspect it was a fake, but at the time it was just about the best thing that had ever happened to me.

One of my all-time favourite sporting memories is the first trip I took with my old man to see Liverpool play in Anfield. The next day we went to the races and picked a winner for Dad out of a field of thirty. I don't even mind that he cheated me out of my winnings ...

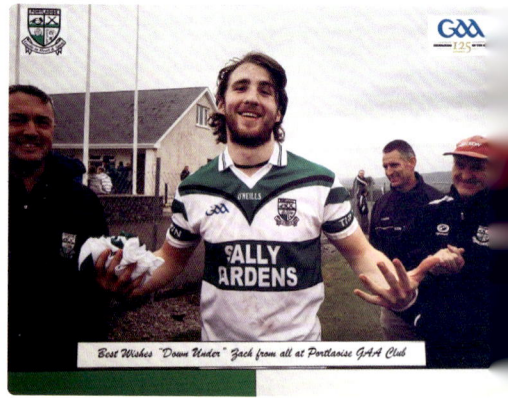

Best Wishes "Down Under" Zach from all at Portlaoise GAA Club

On the left is me playing for Portlaoise, a team I never truly left – even when my AFL career kicked off. On the right is a farewell card from my beloved home team as I took the plunge and headed off to the AFL. (My coaches may or may not have been told I was playing Gaelic Football during some of my off-seasons ...)

Here's my first and only goal *against* Geelong in six years at Carlton. The fast track to playing a new sport at a professional level wasn't easy, but I picked up the Australian game – along with an Australian coffee addiction – quickly enough.

This handsome husky, Olly, was the model for one of my tattoos. I had him to thank for cementing my relationship with my wife, Bec. She kindly offered to look after him while I went home to visit Ireland. This was clearly a blatant attempt to reel me in, but it almost backfired when Olly made a run for it.

An unexpected pregnancy changed everything for us. The first months after Flynn was born in 2013 were so special but also so challenging. At least I wasn't the only one at Carlton wrestling with fatherhood. Here's Flynn and me with my good friend and former housemate Levi Casboult and his oldest son, Lonnie. Levi introduced me and Bec, and he, Hayley and their kids are close friends of ours to this day.

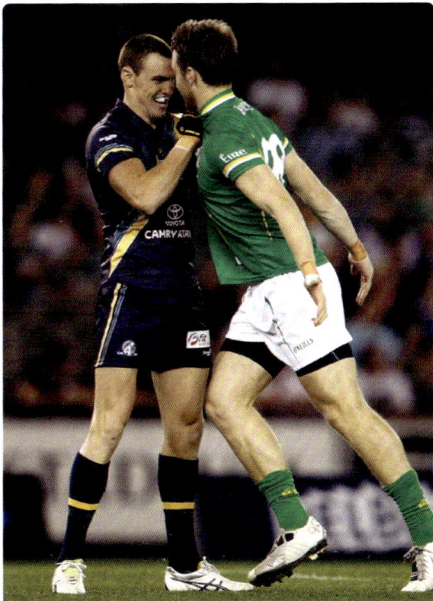

Playing for Ireland in the 2011 International Rules Series was a highlight. A highlight of that highlight was getting into a tussle with my Carlton teammate Mitch Robinson.

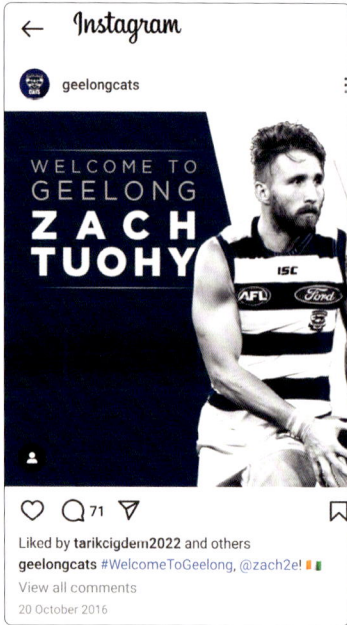

2016 was a year of turmoil for me as I grappled with whether to stay at Carlton and be the one-team player I'd always thought I would be, or to move on. In the end it came down to the wire, and I only learned I had been picked up by Geelong when I saw this Instagram post – complete with what they thought was an Irish flag but was actually the flag of the Ivory Coast. Not the best start – lucky things turned out well anyway!

My nickname 'Reg' is actually a reference to the obscure Harry Potter character Reginald Cattermole and my (alleged) resemblance to the actor who played him (look him up and decide for yourself). Unfortunately it stuck. At least I can impose some of the burden of this nickname on my kids, Flynn and Rafferty.

You might notice I'm not all that cheerful in this photo, despite being chaired off for my 200th game. That's because it was the Covid era of empty stadiums and separated families. Hitting this milestone without Bec and the kids there felt wrong.

In stark contrast to my 200th game, elation doesn't even begin to cover the feeling I had after the 2022 Premiership win. Having Bec and the boys there made it all the sweeter. And with my sister Naomi and my brother-in-law David in the crowd, and the Portlaoise flag around my neck, it felt like a win for my home town as well as for Geelong.

The Cats really embraced the Irish Experiment, and I like to think it paid off. Photos of me with Kerry-born Mark O'Connor after our 2022 Premiership win always make me smile. Incredible that we came across the world to play what was for us an entirely new game, and managed to win one of the biggest prizes the sport has to offer.

My part in the Premiership would never have happened without my parents' support. The win was theirs as much as mine.

You'd think after the Premiership revelry I'd be done with big emotional moments. Obviously not because I had two weddings! On the left you see our modest, efficient, Treasury Building wedding. On the right is a shot from our big-scale wedding party in Ireland – complete with a singsong that lasted much longer than the actual ceremony!

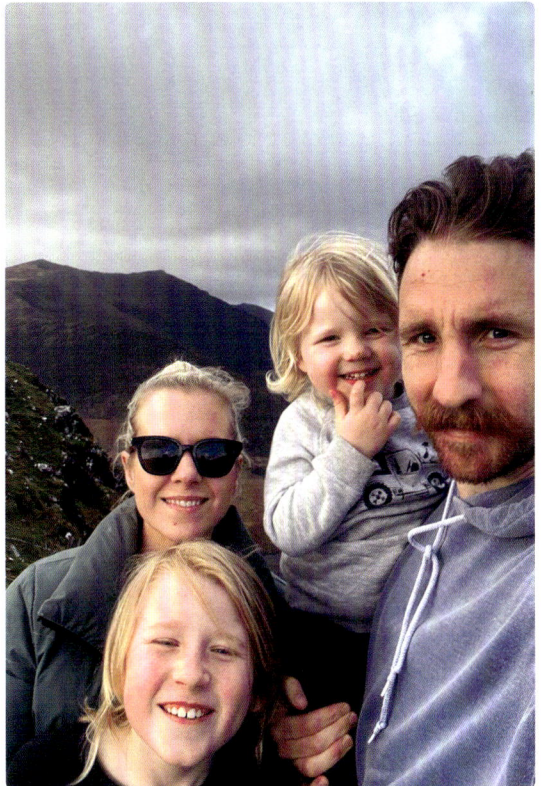

Along with our wedding we got to enjoy a proper trip around my home country with the boys. They'll be Portlaoise boys whether they like it or not.

Retiring was one of the most difficult decisions I've had to make, but I couldn't be prouder of my career, and the time was right to start looking to the future. Also, I'm determined to get at least one more season playing Gaelic football for my home team. The Tuohy clan are headed for Portlaoise.

Bolts, they say communicating is crucial. But communicating is difficult when your 'partner' doesn't want to talk or isn't very skilled at it.

I found Bolts very intense. It was difficult, in fact almost impossible, to have a casual chat with him, about anything unrelated to football. On Monday morning, there was no weekend small talk.

'Hey Bolts, how's things?' you might say as you walked in the door.

He couldn't respond with non-footy chat. It would immediately turn to the match we just played or the plan for the week ahead. And I would think, *Jesus mate, just say 'hi' back and leave it at that. Or make a gag and move on. I didn't ask for a fucking deep and meaningful about where the club is at.* He couldn't turn off for a second.

I started trying to avoid him.

Now if that's what the attempted small talk was like, can you even imagine how meetings were? Let me help you.

The first match we played under Bolts was against his former team, Hawthorn, in the Community Series, as the pre-season competition was called back then. The match was in Launceston, Tasmania, and Bolts was keen to make an impression and to set the tone for how match week and travel would work during his tenure. Little did we know it, but a minor decision on the plane would set the tone for the whole weekend – and perhaps the season.

When we took off from Melbourne, the flight attendants

made their way down the aisle with the refreshments trolley, offering tea or coffee and a biscuit. I had a coffee, skipped the biscuit, and settled in. From memory, the biscuits were those little shortbread tasty morsels. Why do you need to know this? I can explain.

When we arrived at the hotel, we were called into the team room for a meeting. The gathering looked different to when Ratts or Mick had been in charge. All the assistant coaches were in their team gear, even though we weren't planning to leave the building. Bolts had directed them to wear full kit because he wanted everything to feel formal. He wanted them – and us – to know that, even though it was a pre-season game, it was a serious work trip. We weren't there to have fun. It became abundantly clear that there was no fun to be had as soon as we sat down.

'I'd like any player who ate one of the biscuits offered to them on the plane to stand up.'

Now at this point I'm thinking, *Is this a joke? Surely, it's a joke.* But his tone was serious.

Players started to stand up. I couldn't believe what I was seeing. Mostly, I couldn't believe I wasn't one of the ones forced to stand up. It wasn't like me to miss the opportunity of a biscuit. Maybe I hadn't been feeling well.

I was still thinking that this must be some sort of icebreaker or prank.

'Do you think it's professional to do that? Is that going to make you a better player?' Bolts demanded.

Fuck me, it's a biscuit, I thought. A lot of players were standing up.

I couldn't believe what I was seeing and hearing. I got that the guy wanted to set the tone and the standard, but this shit was crazy. It was officially 'Biscuit-gate'.

We lost by 21 points. But all I remember is the shortbread. That incident stayed with me throughout my career. I can't get on a plane, even for a holiday, without thinking about it when I see the trolley.

When we got into the regular season, the level of intensity at meetings made Biscuit-gate look light-hearted.

Round two should have been memorable because when we took on the Sydney Swans at Etihad Stadium, I was playing my 100th game, and my parents had travelled over to watch. But we had lost to Richmond by nine points in round one and, in my milestone match, the Swans thumped us by 60.

Back-to-back losses doesn't make for a very celebratory occasion. Which is a shame. When I first joined the club, Setanta Ó hAilpín had talked to me about what an honour it would be, as an Irish player, to make it to 100 games. Here I was, with 100 matches under my belt, but no one was in the mood to talk about it, including me.

When I was interviewed afterwards, with my parents by my side, I maintained a stern look on my face throughout and kept my answers short. The interviewer's first question was: 'Admittedly, that was a fair old belting, but it must be good to have your parents here?' Or something like that.

Yep, it was a 'fair old belting', in more ways than one.

Swans' superstar, Buddy Franklin, slung me into the turf in a tackle just as the half-time siren went and, in anger, when I made it back to my feet, I shoved him. This instigated a bit of an all-in wrestle as players rushed to join. It all occurred right in front of the Sydney Swans' cheer squad.

Now here I was being interviewed about that melee, in front of my parents, after my 100th match. Good times.

But at Carlton, it seemed things could always get worse, and they did.

We lost to the Gold Coast Suns by 54 points at Metricon Stadium in round three. When we assembled for the match review, the atmosphere was tense. On the occasion of a particularly rough review, John Barker would say to us on the way into the meeting room, 'Put your seatbelts on.' This was his way of lightening the mood, while warning us that we needed to be ready for some direct feedback.

Despite the loss, Sam Docherty had shot the lights out. As we all knew, he was an elite player and he had played an unbelievable game, even by his lofty standards. Sam isn't just one of the best footballers I've played with, he's also one of the best people. Inspired by his epic performance, Bolts decided that the mantra for the meeting would be 'What would Doch do?'

In theory, this sounds good, right?

A superstar of the club getting the acknowledgement he deserved for a good performance in a loss. I mean, it's easy to play well when you're thrashing a team, but to keep your standards high in a loss is impressive.

Bolts ran through every aspect of our game and, after each aspect, he would more or less ask, 'Why can't you all play like Sam?'

The meeting consisted of a series of highlights of Sam's (there were plenty to choose from), followed by a lowlight from one of his teammates.

At one point in the meeting, Bolts drew our attention to a video that highlighted what he perceived to be a lowlight. It involved not only me but Sam too. *Perfect for this meeting, very on-brand*, I thought.

I was in a stoppage (this is a ball-up or throw-in) and the ball was bouncing around, but I managed to gain possession. Doch had run around on the outside and I went to give it to him, but a Gold Coast player, Aaron Hall I think, dove to intercept, so I quickly changed course and kicked it forward. A different Gold Coast player intercepted – I had caused a turnover. I thought nothing of it during the match because I believed I had taken the only safe option, even though it didn't work out. It turns out Bolts had not dismissed it so easily.

'Why didn't you pass the ball to Doch?' he asked.

I just wanted this part of the meeting to be over, so I responded quickly and, in a way, I thought he'd be pleased with what I said and, therefore, move on. 'Actually, looking at it now, I should have tried to squeeze it through to him, as he's made such a good run. I wanted to give it to him, but I thought the Gold Coast player had read it and would intercept if I tried to squeeze it through, so I just reacted to that and tried to kick it forward.'

I thought this response was satisfactory, but Bolts wasn't having any of it. He continued to pursue it. Johnny Barker was trying to interrupt to defend me, but Bolts wouldn't let him speak.

'I wanted to give it, I was trying to give it,' I insisted in a bid to quell his concerns about my game management and end what I thought was a pretty futile conversation about a minuscule detail of the game.

But he wasn't listening. He was fuming. It wasn't enough that he was talking me down. He decided to open it up to the group. He started asking my teammates what they thought, including a player who was a hero of mine back then – I still think the world of him.

'What do you reckon?' he said to Kade Simpson.

'It's tough but, yes, he should just give it next time,' Simmo responded.

Simmo really should have told him that, no, he was wrong. But he probably wanted this ordeal to be over just as much as I did. I don't blame him. No one was going to stick up for me. As we watched my alleged misdemeanour in super-slow motion and I pointed out that I only had a millisecond to make the decision, it all fell on deaf ears.

I'm not opposed to this sort of postmortem after a loss. This is the stuff that good teams talk about all the time. But there's a constructive way to do it. For example, a coach could instruct you that next time, you should give that handball, even if there's an element of risk. The coach could explain that if they end up turning it over and they score a goal, we'll cop it, because we know that, for every goal they kick, we'll kick five because we're giving those handballs.

If he'd said something like that I would have been like: 'Okay, that's what we're doing from now on.' And I'd have followed that instruction to the letter.

But there was nothing constructive about that meeting. A Doch highlight, then a lowlight. Then the pivotal question. 'Doch wouldn't do this, so why did you?'

Over and over.

Sam was sitting near me. He was mortified by the whole process. He'd had no idea this was going to happen before the meeting started. He looked like he needed a seatbelt for different reasons as he was squirming in his seat so much it could have caused an injury.

If Doch hadn't been so loved by his teammates, this could have been a really good way to divide the team. It could have ended very badly, and he would have been completely isolated from the group. But his character and popularity meant this meeting didn't result in that worst-case scenario.

Johnny Barker had been trying to interject during the interaction between me and Bolts. He had lined up another teammate, Marc Murphy if I remember correctly was in a very similar situation where he had tried to give a handball to another player, not to Doch on this occasion, and it was intercepted. The result was worse than in my situation, because at least if you kick the ball forward and it's intercepted, the opposition has to come back through traffic. If you do that in a stoppage and it's intercepted, you're in trouble. Barks wanted to use this as an example of how these decisions are not black and white and can go either way, like a good coach does. But Bolts wouldn't let him show it.

I was furious. I've never been so angry after a meeting. It was round three and I officially knew: Bolts wasn't into me.

I've copped sprays from coaches over the journey – senior coaches, assistant coaches, VFL coaches – they've all had a go and it's never felt personal. This was the only time in my 15-year career that I've sat in a meeting and thought, *This bloke just has it in for me.*

My approach from that day onwards was to just try to get through the year. I couldn't help but think about the irony of our pre-season chat. Remember I mentioned him asking what the club needed to do to be better and I suggested that we start with not being so fucking miserable?

I can confirm that I've never, ever, dreaded going to work as much as I did when Brendon Bolton was in charge of the club.

The only thing worse than a group meeting with Bolts was a one-on-one meeting. And Bolts loved to line up meetings.

On one occasion, he set up a get-together that involved a senior player and one of the younger players going into his office to look through video clips of games. I was paired up with Jacob Weitering for one of these meetings. We looked at some of his plays, and they were largely positive, with Bolts offering a few coaching notes.

Bolts was actually a great coach, but his communication style was lacking. At the end of the meeting, he turned away from Jacob and looked at me. 'Do you have any feedback for me as a coach?'

That is when I made a fatal mistake. You see, I assumed that when he asked me for feedback, he wanted, well, feedback. In reality, what he wanted, it seems to me now, was to be told how fantastic he was. Unfortunately, I had misinterpreted the question and instead I responded with, you guessed it – real feedback.

'Things are going great, but I do get the impression that some of the younger players are intimidated by you. I don't feel like they're comfortable speaking to you,' I offered politely.

Silence. And then some more of it.

Silence is awkward.

I spoke up. I needed it to end.

'As I said, things are really great, I just don't think many of the younger blokes would be willing to knock on your door for a chat if it wasn't an organised thing … like this.'

He … was … fuming.

I knew it when I left the office but confirmation quickly followed.

An hour later, John Barker approached me. 'What did you say to Bolts? Because he is filthy with you. He's in his office, chewing his lips off.'

Oh no, I really had interpreted his question wrongly. Things weren't good between us, obviously, and my feedback wasn't going to help.

A week later, he was clearly still overthinking it and he brought it up in a team meeting, in what he thought was a positive framing. To me it felt so staged. I still don't know if he was trying to make me feel better or make himself look good.

'So, I asked Zach for feedback in a meeting, and he gave me feedback that I wasn't ready for at the time. I didn't want to hear it but now I've processed it, and it was good feedback to hear.'

At the time, I was thinking, *I can't read the guy at all. Is it all for show or does he mean this?*

While he seemed to be trying to make the point that he was over it, it didn't feel that way. He was frosty with me, at best, but sometimes under pressure things would really blow up.

One of those times was during a half-time meeting at Etihad Stadium, when we were losing. We lost a lot that year so it's difficult to remember which particular beating this was, but I was sitting in my usual spot when he yelled at me.

I had entered the room to find my seat in the back corner, furthest away from the door. That's where I always sit in meetings and continued to do so until the end of my career. I was sitting next to one of our assistants, who was talking second-half tactics. Bolts had started his half-time speech but I hadn't realised, because I was bending down to tie my laces.

'Zach, look at me when I'm talking to you,' he bellowed. That was the teacher in him.

All right, Dad, calm down, I thought. *I'm not five years old.*

I did not say this. Luckily. He was red with anger; things had the potential to escalate further if I responded at all. I knew my place. I was third fiddle behind Doch and Kade Simpson. He adored Doch, who was captain, and Simmo was a club legend, and then there was me, who he didn't even like. The problem was, I was increasingly getting the feeling that Bolts didn't even consider me worthy of playing third fiddle.

Things were bleak, which was ironic, as the phrase Bolts loved to use to summarise our approach to the season was 'blue skies'.

All AFL clubs decide on a mantra at the start of the year. They have a meeting and talk about their objectives and goals for the season and come up with a phrase that best represents that. One of our 2016 catch cries was 'blue skies' – which I think was meant to signify clarity of mind and good decision-making, etc. Bolts, being the intense bloke that he is, really took this seriously. He had a meeting with the whole club to decide it. Everyone from the team doctor to the head of membership was there. I'm not sure if the team doctor at the time, whose only focus was keeping us healthy, knew why he had been included. But 'blue skies' is what emerged – and it was used repetitively at all club meetings.

The famous catchphrase even started to creep into Bolts' media interviews. I cringed every time I saw it in print. After I left, the phrase was 'green shoots', and you might recall when Bolts went down the slide at the 'Big Freeze' fundraiser, he brought a watering can and said, 'I've just got to keep watering those green shoots at the Blues.' He was obsessive like that. Another example of how he couldn't switch off.

At the end of the 2016 season, which wasn't a good one, we finished fourteenth on the ladder with a 7–15 win–loss ratio.

I knew things between me and Bolts had gone absolutely tits-up. I was out of contract when I went to a meeting with him and Neil Craig. Neil was director of coaching, development and performance at the time, and I was a big fan of his. They wanted to know why I hadn't signed my contract extension. I assured them I didn't want to leave; I just wasn't happy with the particulars of my contract.

During the course of this meeting, Neil complimented

me. 'I notice you've got better at receiving feedback, which is great.'

'Oh really?' I responded.

I always thought I was quite good at that but, obviously, Bolts did not think it was one of my strong points.

'For example, remember that meeting during the year, where you kept biting back at Bolts?'

Oh. My. God. I thought. *He's bringing up the Doch meeting again.* Were they trying to rile me up? Were they testing me again? And then there was the irony of Bolts overthinking my feedback that he didn't like for a whole week, so much so he made the next team meeting about it.

I didn't want to leave the Blues; I had been happy there until that year. But how could Bolts and I move forward if this was how it was going to be?

As well as the issues I was experiencing with Bolts, I had major concerns about my new contract. They were offering me a two-year extension, but with match payments. The way this sort of AFL deal works is that you get a base wage and then you're paid a sum for every match you play on top of that. This is a great deal if you're on the periphery of the team and you manage to secure a regular spot. Match payments were about $4,000 back then, so it adds up if you work your way in. For more established players, who play every game, it is more common for the contract to be for a single, higher wage.

At this point, I hadn't missed a game for four seasons. I had played every match since round one in 2013. If I hadn't missed a match for years, why were they doing this? The match payments component was raising major red flags and my manager, Adam 'Rama' Ramanauskas, agreed.

What their offer told me was that maybe they didn't see me as a regular, and they were planning to save money. To me, it felt like Bolts didn't think he'd be selecting me every week.

Although I didn't want to take the contract as it was, on the balance of things, I didn't want to leave Carlton. I'd started my career there.

Rama went back to them and said, 'Tally up the match payments for the season, add it to the base and he's willing to take slightly less than that to make it work. He doesn't want to leave.'

They refused to adjust the offer. At this point, I knew it: Bolts really didn't like me. All my friendly advances, all that relationship-building and effort, had got me nowhere.

I had to start thinking about other options.

As it happened, North Melbourne had approached me earlier in the season. I had met them at Arden Street Oval. They had snuck Rama and me in the back door, after the offices had closed down for the day. It had all been very clandestine – and that had made it exciting. I liked that they had approached me and they were really keen. In the meeting, they had sold the club to me, not the other way around.

I was very flattered, as a club had never courted me like that before. Added to that, I had always been a fan of the North Melbourne coach, Brad Scott. He was sometimes confrontational in media interviews, but, when he was, it was always in defence of his players, and I liked that about him.

I was so impressed with him that when, shortly after the meeting at Arden Street, Michael Voss was sacked as coach of Brisbane and Brad was linked to the vacant job, I rang up Rama to tell him that if Brad Scott was not at North Melbourne, I wouldn't consider going there.

North was offering me a three-year contract and significantly more money than Carlton. But, despite everything, my gut instinct was telling me that I should still be aiming to be a one-club player.

Carlton was only offering two years and – still – only match payments. They assured me I could take my time while making the decision.

During this time, my mind often went to Geelong. If there was a team I'd be willing to give up my one-club player ambition for, it was them. Their reputation preceded them, and I was fully aware of the programme they ran at the Cattery. Not to mention their record of consistent success, and the fact I wanted to win a flag. I'd never been shy about stating my goal to win a Premiership. But I didn't know how it all worked. Could I get my manager to just call them up?

What worked in my favour is that my good friend Lachie Henderson had left Carlton for Geelong the year before. I'd asked him to start dropping my name around the club. I was half-joking, but kind of hoping he would oblige. In fact, he did more than I asked. He went into Stephen Wells (the club's head of recruitment) to put my name forward.

Despite this, I hadn't heard anything from them. What I learned was that their interest in recruiting me was dependent on whether Corey Enright retired or not. My footy fate was hanging on the decision of an opposition player. It felt weird willing someone to retire (sorry, Corey!), but the more I thought about Geelong, the more I felt like it would be the right option for me.

In the end, I was on an end-of-season golf trip with none other than Hendo when some welcome news popped up on his phone. We were in the same golf buggy driving to the next hole on the beautiful Jack's Point Golf Course in Queenstown when he saw a notification on the Geelong players' WhatsApp group. Corey Enright had messaged the boys.

'Hey guys, letting you know I've decided to retire.'

The two of us were in the golf cart thinking, *Please, please can the Cattery call right now?* Boris (Corey's nickname) –

you legend. Thanks for retiring. Sorry again! I feel bad that I celebrated your retirement but I was desperate to move clubs.

But my phone stayed silent, at least from a Geelong point of view, for the rest of the trip. When I got home, Rama called me.

'I have good news and bad news,' he said. 'The good news is, Geelong has called. They haven't put forward anything official yet, but they seem keen. The bad news is, Carlton has refused to improve their offer or change the match payments situation. Which I think is disrespectful to you.'

I was furious with the Blues. Not long before that, CEO Steven Trigg had spoken about my contract in the media and claimed they had put forward a good offer but that I was slow to sign.

A good offer? Are you fucking kidding me?

I agreed with Rama. It was all so disrespectful. Even if I took their crappy offer and stayed at the club, fans would think I wanted to leave anyway and might turn against me. North Melbourne's interest in signing me had made news and, coupled with Trigg's comments, they'd already be doubting my intentions and loyalty.

There and then, I made my decision. Even if the Cats offered a worse contract than Carlton had offered, I would take it. My gut was telling me that Geelong was the place for me.

At the Blues, I wasn't valued by the coach or the club, so I was done.

Rama organised a meeting with Geelong's coach, Chris Scott, the general manager of footy at the time, Steve Hocking, and the head of recruitment, Stephen Wells.

To say he was 'head of recruitment' is underselling Stephen Wells. Wellsy was regarded as a recruitment guru. He was responsible for the signing of Gary Ablett Junior, Jimmy Bartel, Paul Chapman, Steve Johnson and a host of other star players. I was aware of the level of talent he had dealt with in his time and I was nervous to be in a room with the three of them.

Chris Scott was the twin brother of Brad Scott, the North Melbourne coach I'd been so impressed by. Unlike the meeting I'd had with Brad, I was very much selling myself to Chris and the club, rather than the other way around. They were interviewing me to see if I was a good fit. We met in the boardroom of an apartment block – unlike at North Melbourne, where we'd been snuck in after hours. Rama was there too.

Chris asked why I wanted to leave Carlton.

'I really don't feel valued there. And I'm worried about the longevity of my career if I don't go to a club that matches the ambition I have,' I said.

I was desperate to impress and I was pleased with how it went. I could tell that they liked me.

By now, it was public knowledge that North Melbourne

was interested in me, but Chris seemed comfortable meeting up with me nonetheless.

What I didn't know at the time was that Brad owned property in the apartment block we met in. He had loaned the keys to Chris for the meeting, who had proceeded to use the facilities to interview a player his brother had also wanted to lure to his club. That's how the Scott brothers roll, I guess. They're all business.

Down the track, I asked Chris if Brad knew we were meeting at the time.

'Of course he did,' he said nonchalantly.

Shortly after the meeting, I packed up and went to Ireland with Bec and Flynn to see the family. Leaving the country with no contract offer was unsettling to say the least. But it was just the way it had to be.

Having decided that North Melbourne probably wasn't for me, another club had come into the equation. When I landed in Dublin, I had a voicemail from Rama. The Gold Coast Suns had got in touch and they were willing to offer far more than North Melbourne. When I say more, I mean more in every sense – money and contract duration.

A few days later, Geelong came through with an offer, which was, of course, dependent on the club negotiating a successful trade with Carlton.

For readers not familiar with the trade period, which takes place shortly after the end of the season, clubs can agree to trade players who want to leave, but if they don't get what they want in return for their personnel (this includes player swaps and/or draft picks), players can end up stranded where they are, and sometimes out of favour.

Geelong's offer was higher than Carlton's, but significantly lower than both North Melbourne and the Gold Coast Suns.

I didn't want to go to the Gold Coast. It would mean uprooting my family, but I had to consider it. I had a young family and it would be wrong not to think about it. The Gold Coast offer wasn't just more money, it was also for an extra year, with each year's salary increasing incrementally. It was tempting from a security point of view. I'd gone from Carlton only offering a base salary and match payments to the Gold Coast Suns offering it all to get me over the line.

I asked my friend Kieran Lillis for advice over a pint. Kieran was playing for Laois at the time and, in case you're not aware, I should point out that Gaelic football is completely amateur. There is no money, just expenses if you're lucky and sponsorship perks at the top teams, though there's not many of those at Laois. I took him through all my options. Kieran seemed blinded by the dollar signs on offer.

'Go to the Gold Coast, you'd be mad not to,' he said.

He wasn't the only one advising me to go. Pearce Hanley, a former Mayo Gaelic footballer, also called me. He was about to be traded to the Gold Coast Suns from the Brisbane Lions. He told me that he had gone through the facility and it was extremely impressive. Even the coach at the time,

Rodney Eade, made contact. Just like Brad Scott had at North, he was really selling the club to me. Between the financial offer and the fact I felt wanted by a coach for the first time in a long time, it was tempting.

But something inside me knew that Geelong was the right choice. I was desperate to win a Premiership. I thought about the days I used to look through Carlton's list before I even moved to Australia, to try to predict when they could win that elusive Premiership. It had always been my goal. If I was going to stay true to that, then it would have to be Geelong.

I rang Rama and said, if Geelong can just add another year to my contract – a fourth year – I'm in. Despite the fact it was significantly lower money, I just knew it was where I wanted to be. Geelong agreed to that straightaway.

When I made the final call on it, I was with Levi Casboult and his future wife Hayley, and Sam Docherty and his future wife Nat. They were visiting Ireland and staying with Bec and me at my family home. We were out on the Saturday night before trade week started, at Lilly's where I had originally signed my contract with Carlton. Rama called me to confirm that he was about to go public with my request to go to the Cattery and lodge the official paperwork. I walked outside to talk to him.

It was a massive decision and the reality of it, as well as the finality of knowing I was going to leave Carlton – while my two teammates were visiting my family in Portlaoise – hit me hard. When I went back inside, they knew I was really upset. I'm emotional at the best of times, but we had been out for a good part of the evening already, so let's just say I was more emotional than usual.

There I was, sitting in the exact location where I had signed my first contract and now I'd decided to leave the club. When I first signed that paper with Steven Icke, I would never have thought that, years later, I would be in the same spot but choosing to leave. Signing that first professional contract was one of the best moments of my life. Now it was over with the Blues.

I had always wanted to be a one-club player, and now I knew it wasn't going to happen. In Ireland, you can't swap clubs or counties. You play for the town you are born in and the county you grow up in. There are no transfers, unless in very unusual circumstances, and when it does happen it's frowned upon. Loyalty was in my blood and I'd never imagined moving. But Bolts had pushed me out and I had to get on with it.

I think I've made it obvious that Bolts and I never jived. However, I do think he was a good teacher of the game and his work ethic was never in question. Since leaving the Blues, he's gone on to enjoy success at Collingwood as part of the coaching team that won the 2023 Premiership.

In fact, I've yet to meet a player who has a bad word to say about him as an assistant. But being an assistant coach versus a senior coach has one major difference. As an assistant coach, you can be friends with players – it's a lot more challenging as a senior coach. It's important that there's some sort of distance there. Maybe he just didn't know how to achieve that, how to find a middle ground. And that's okay. Some guys are just not meant to be senior coaches. He's clearly a great assistant. I'm just unfortunate that he was my senior coach.

Despite my difficulty with Bolts, the decision to leave went against everything I believed in. I was petrified that I wasn't making the right call. It was all too much, so I went outside and cried privately.

When I came back in, the group was worried about the night going downhill fast. I mean, I had to excuse myself to go and have a moment, which is never a good sign on a night out.

My friends took action. They organised a tray of shots – from memory they were baby Guinness – and they spelled out my initials. My name was on them so I did what any decent person would do and drank the majority of them. As you can imagine, the night escalated to the point where I was a lot more relaxed about my career move.

The recovery took almost as long as the trade to Geelong did. Over a week later, I still hadn't heard anything and I was getting anxious. There were only a few days of trade left. I was texting Rama: 'What the fuck is going on here, mate?'

In the end, I found out about my move via Instagram. The Cats had tagged me in a post. Of course, Rama had called me and left a voicemail but I woke up one morning and the first thing I saw was the Insta notification.

The post was memorable for a few reasons. Firstly, they had taken an action shot of me and Photoshopped on the Geelong colours – it was weird to see myself in the Hoops for the first time. '#WelcomeToGeelong @zach2e', said the caption. With a flag alongside it that they thought was an Irish flag.

In fact, it was the Ivory Coast flag. Same colours, different order. I'm surprised I noticed as I had only just woken up. My family and I laughed so hard at that. I didn't let the social-media team live it down for a while.

I was officially a Geelong player. The Cats gave up their first-round draft pick, as well as forward Billie Smedts and draft pick number 63 (the annual draft is about new or unsigned players joining AFL clubs). In return, they got a future second-round draft pick and, of course, me.

They had shown faith in me and I was going to repay it. No matter what.

CHAPTER 7

Coming Home
to the Cattery

MY FIRST MATCH FOR GEELONG WAS A PRE-SEASON
clash against Hawthorn in Launceston, in the lead-up to the
2017 season.

There I was, sitting on the plane next to my teammates
at the start of my first interstate trip, with a myriad of
catastrophic thoughts going through my mind. What if I
play badly? What if I have a bad year? Even worse, what if
we all have a bad year and finish low down the ladder and
the future first-round draft pick they swapped as part of my
deal is wasted?

I'd always wanted to be a running half-back but, at Carlton, I'd never been permitted to fill that role. I was behind Sam Docherty and Kade Simpson in the pecking order. But it was clear during pre-season that the Cats wanted me to be exactly that. What if I couldn't pull it off, even though I'd always wanted to do it?

Then there was the interstate trip dynamic to navigate. When flying, the club books all the business-class seats available, as well as premium economy and exit rows. There's a hierarchy involved in how those seats are designated.

The most experienced and tallest players at the club get the business-class seats, which makes sense. The rest of us spread out in the exit/premium aisles. You can imagine my horror when, on an early flight with the club, Joel Selwood walked past me sitting in business class to take a seat in an exit row down the back. I was mortified and begged him to swap with me. Clearly there had been a mistake, made by the airline no doubt, as the club wouldn't send Joel down the back?

'Joel, this is wrong!' I pleaded. 'I'm a first-year player with the club. I shouldn't be here.'

But Joel didn't care about stuff like that. He just laughed and proceeded to his seat.

On this particular flight to Launceston, I was in a suitable seat – premium economy, not business. I had managed the seating situation and the pre-match butterflies, so far.

Then something terrifying happened.

A flight attendant was veering towards us with a broad smile. I could hear it before I could see it – those miniature bottles of wine clinking against one another as the trolley moved perilously close to where I was sitting.

And I could only think about one thing – Biscuit-gate.

The great Patrick Dangerfield was only a few seats away. But all I could focus on was the dreaded refreshments trolley advancing towards me ominously.

When I saw what was on offer, I shuddered.

This was an even greater test than the one I'd faced at the Blues, and one that surely would have ramifications if I got it wrong. Forget shortbread! Delicious little pots of fluffy chocolate mousse were being cheerfully handed out by the flight attendants. Chris Scott didn't seem like the kind of coach who would allow something so petty to bother him, but I had become somewhat institutionalised under the Bolton regime and wasn't about to take any risks. I wasn't going to be brought down by chocolate mousse so early into my Geelong tenure.

When asked if I wanted one of those delightful little pots of joy, I replied with a firm, 'No way.' *You'll have to do better than chocolate mousse, Scotty*, I thought.

I was feeling really good about myself.

Then I glanced over at Patrick Dangerfield just a few seats away from me – now bear in mind this guy is a generational talent and the AFL's best player at the time – and there he was, knuckles deep into his second mousse.

Still scarred by Biscuit-gate, I thought this was an elaborate plot to take down the new signing. What if Scotty and Danger had orchestrated this? What if I had one little chocolate mousse and was then castigated for not knowing my place on the team?

It wasn't until our pre-match meeting on arrival at the hotel passed without any mention of chocolate mousse that I realised things were different at the Cats. I've had a good laugh with Chris Scott about Biscuit-gate since then, and my plane-trolley phobia has become a running gag at the club.

In addition to permitting players to indulge in chocolate mousse, the club was incredibly friendly. As soon as I was signed – while I was still in Europe – my phone lit up with WhatsApp messages from players welcoming me to the club. When you get traded, your phone number is sent out to the squad, and they didn't wait long to use it.

Bec and I had flown from Ireland to Amsterdam for a few days with Sam (Docherty) and Natalie, and I remember sitting at the train station there looking through the messages and responding to as many as I could.

There were about 30 notifications – they just kept coming. I couldn't believe it. It was so strange to be there in Amsterdam with a Carlton legend like Doch, who, all of a sudden, was not my teammate, and to be corresponding with these Geelong guys – one of whom I'd had a major run-in with on the field when I was wearing Carlton colours.

I replied to Joel Selwood straightaway, and not just because of the aforementioned run-in. It was surreal that he now had my phone number.

Joel and I, infamously, had clashed back in 2013. The Blues played the Cats in round three at Etihad Stadium. Just before the halftime siren sounded, Joel and I were in a contest. Joel felt like he should have got a free kick for head-high contact (I know, who'd have thought … if you know, you know). He was politely asking the umpire why he didn't award it.

Being the good Samaritan that I am, I went over to make sure he was okay, which is my way of saying I went over and started calling him all kinds of names. I was asking him if his little face was okay in a really patronising tone, and he didn't like it much. One thing led to another, and then – whack – Joel slapped me. Right across the face. He slapped the shit out of me.

A lot happens on the field but I had never been slapped before. That was a first. My beard was thick at that point and it cushioned the blow. When I look back on it, I think I deserved it, and some more. I had been coached to niggle, both back home and in Australia, and my attempts to antagonise had got an eye-catching response this time. I look back at the absolute fuck-wittery of what I used to do and think I would have slapped me too.

We can laugh about it now, but even with our strong bond as Premiership teammates, it is still one of my favourite bits of video footage to pull up on my phone whenever I get the opportunity. In fact, I've posted it on my social media a couple of times to celebrate Joel's milestones. It never gets old.

The other name that really jumped out at me as I scrolled through my phone was Matthew Scarlett. To get a message from that legend was huge. To me, he epitomised everything that Geelong was – all the traits that made me want to move to the club.

And the messages were just the start of it. The in-person welcomes I got when I arrived at the club were even better.

I started training as soon as I got back from my trip to Ireland. As the younger players return to pre-season before the senior players, I didn't get to meet many of those big names for the first couple of weeks.

On my first day, I was haunted by the old Carlton regime and the Melbourne traffic I had contended with for years. Between my early days in the Honda Civic, Levi 'borrowing' my car from time to time and congested streets, I had got into the habit of leaving for work early because I was terrified of being late.

I would leave my house at 6 a.m. and, when Flynn started going to childcare, I would drop him off when it opened at 6.30 a.m. This made for an anxious start to the day as, if traffic was bad, it might mean I was late for training. Added to that, Flynn didn't love being dropped off and would sometimes cry when I left him there. That killed me. Seeing his little eyes fill with tears and then having to rush off made for a very stressful start to the day.

On my first day of training, I left our house in Herne Hill in Geelong about an hour before I needed to be at the club. We had just relocated from Melbourne and hadn't found a creche for Flynn yet, so I was headed straight there. I wanted them to see how keen I was. Approximately 10 minutes later, I arrived at my new workplace.

Great, I thought, *I'll go in and get settled. Maybe even do a longer warm-up.*

The only problem was, the club was locked up. No one else had arrived yet. Not even the staff.

I ended up having to climb a fence onto the oval and then enter the race so I could knock on doors in an attempt to gain access to the locker room. I walked around for half an hour but not even the cleaners were there to let me in.

Now, you'd think that the first day would have taught me a lesson. Surely, I could set my alarm a little later? Oh, no. Still scarred by the Blues regime, I continued to arrive up to an hour early, every single day. For weeks. I would be waiting for the physios when they arrived for work. They would look at me and laugh.

'This isn't Carlton, mate. You don't need to rock up so early,' they chuckled.

A bit like Biscuit-mousse-gate, my teammates still joke

about it. It took time for me to adjust to a much more relaxed Cats' way.

Matthew Scarlett, whose name had jolted me when it first appeared on my phone in Amsterdam, was one of the first coaches I met. We had a clinic down at the beach and he was there. He walked straight over to introduce himself.

'When I first heard that the club might be getting you, Zach, I was really excited. I'm pumped you're here,' he said.

At least that's how I remember it. When someone you admire so much is saying words like these to you, it all gets a little bit blurry. I couldn't believe someone of his status at the club would offer that encouragement.

Putting the jumper (AFL jersey) on for the first time provided a big dose of reality. They needed a photo of me in my new kit, so I went into the change room to put it on. Looking in the mirror and seeing those hoops was weird. It was like my face didn't match it – I was so used to the navy blue. It shouldn't have felt strange as I had wanted to move there so much. Geelong, out of all my options, was the club I was desperate to go to, and now it had happened.

Looking back, the trepidation probably came from a fear of it not working out. What if I wasn't the player they thought I was? Getting used to those hoops was going to take some time.

One of the first tasks on my to-do list when the senior players returned to training was to ask Joel Selwood out for coffee. I had a feeling, because of the well-documented slap he'd given me, that he might, in fact, think I was a bit of a tool. I thought it was best to buy him a coffee and explain that I was not, in fact, a tool. We met at 63 Degrees café and sat in a booth out the back.

All I really wanted to do was make sure Joel knew I was there for the right reasons. Joel is someone I respect more than I can adequately articulate.

Regardless of how good you think he was as a player or how influential you think he was as a captain, I can assure you his impact was even greater than you can imagine. Everything Joel ever did on or off the field was for the betterment of the Cats. I needed him to know that I was going to try to bring real value to the club. That I was only motivated by success – that, to me, Geelong wasn't just a pit stop on the way to the end of my career. That I was here to try and make the club better and hopefully help us win a flag someday.

More often than you think, players move to clubs and all they do is see out their first contract on the journey to retirement. Often, they realise they're a poor fit – if the club doesn't first – and it doesn't work out well for either party. I was desperate to ensure that wouldn't be my story.

Joel was there when I arrived. It was weird to see him away from the club, in his civvies. It was the first time I'd seen him in a social environment.

He was calm and relaxed as always. I was trying to contend with Flynn, who was two years old and very energetic. We put him on the inside of the booth, in a bid to contain him so we could talk.

We started with small talk. He asked me how I was finding the place. I think he was aware that I had something I wanted to bring to his attention. But I only had one thing to say.

'I'm in it for the long haul and I really want to add value. I want to achieve success and I'll work hard for that,' I said.

Joel was brilliant and reassured me that I had nothing to worry about. He is every bit the legend you think he is (if you're a Cats fan – if you're not, you might not like him because, deep down, you wish he'd been on your team). Even though I knew he must like me enough – I had no doubt that if he didn't want me traded to the club, he could have vetoed it – it felt good to have that discussion openly.

You might think it's exaggerated just how good a captain Joel Selwood was, but it's not. I've never met anyone so invested in a club. And when I say the club, I mean he was involved in everything. For Joel, training and playing would only make up 50 per cent of his job, if even that. The hours he put in were huge and he had time for everyone.

I had squared things off with the skipper early on. Now, I could focus on really important issues in my new workplace. Top of that list was that I had a new nickname to get used to. Everyone at the Cattery was calling me 'Reg'.

As most people will be aware, you don't get to choose your nickname. I'll add to that by saying, in Australia, if you are christened with a new nickname and you rally against it, it sticks even harder. Do you have any influence at all on how that nickname is chosen in the first place? Absolutely not.

Technically, it wasn't actually new.

The nickname 'Reg' had come about on a post-season golf trip to Queenstown in New Zealand in 2015 with Ciarán Sheehan, Dennis Armfield, Matt Dick, Sam Docherty and Lachie Henderson, who had just made his move to the Cats.

I had that really long beard at the time and decided, while I was there, to visit a barber and get it shaved off. I kept my moustache of course; I had become very attached to that, and still am to this day.

After my visit to the barber, I FaceTimed Bec, who thankfully approved of my new look. How could she not love the moustache staying? She's only human. But what would the boys think? After Bec, their opinion holds most weight.

I turned up to the pub looking for feedback. I didn't get much. The boys were, understandably, more interested in ensuring our drinks order was sorted. Then we started talking about nicknames, and I casually mentioned I'd never had one. It'd always just been 'Tuohy'. No one had put any effort into anything original. After a reasonably poor round of golf and a few nice red wines, out of nowhere Sam Docherty piped up.

'You're Reg! You're Reg!'

I searched my mind for a really handsome moustache-bearing Reg that he could be drawing inspiration from, but no one came to mind. When I sought clarification, I got the feedback I'd been seeking since my visit to the barber's.

'You know Reginald Cattermole?' he laughed. 'From Harry Potter? You're identical.'

I googled his image and was initially in denial. I had hoped this Reginald would be a handsome devil.

'It's the big nose and the moustache,' Doch explained. 'It's you!'

No offence to the actor that plays him, Steffan Rhodri, but I had thought of myself as more Hugh Jackman-esque. It's fair to say this was a dent to the ego. I should have limited my feedback requests to just Bec.

As it happened, the name didn't stick straightaway. Our night was big, and maybe Doch didn't remember his ingenious idea. But Hendo took it and ran with it. He changed my name in his phone to 'Reggie' and, a year later when I joined the Cats, I was welcomed in as that. Reggie. I can still remember the giggles from Hendo in our team meetings every time Scotty would refer to me as Reg. Simple pleasures.

Aside from the absolute necessity to have a nickname at the Cattery, what struck me immediately about the culture of Geelong was the family vibe and the genuine care that players showed each other. I experienced this early on. In the December of my first pre-season, Olly, my dog who I have inked on my skin and who helped Bec and me cement our relationship, died.

I was devastated. Olly had been by my side since I'd bought him from a breeder in Ballarat four years earlier. When I had walked into the breeder's house, Olly had run straight up to me – and we had barely been apart since. He had the run of our house and was permitted to sleep in our bed, if he wanted. Although Olly was very independent and didn't always want to. He had his own bed downstairs and would sleep there if he needed space, but if he fancied a morning snuggle, he knew he could come into our room.

You've heard about his escape-artist tactics, but his yearning for freedom meant that, in his later years, he was quite difficult to get home from the park. One night, I was very close to leaving him there in the dark. I was shouting his name and he wouldn't come back to me. But Olly couldn't resist new people, so when a couple walked past, I asked for their help. They kindly lured him back to me by walking in his direction. When he bounded up to meet them, they grabbed him by the collar and returned him to me. I put him on the floor of the passenger seat of my car gave him a stern talk on the way home. But he was a beautiful dog, so it was hard to be angry with him for long.

Bec, Flynn and I had just returned from our trip to Ireland. Olly had been staying with Bec's mum and dad in Bendigo when he fell really ill. The vets had no idea what was wrong with him, but I loved that dog so much I was willing to do and/or pay anything to try to help him. They transferred him from Bendigo to Werribee Animal Hospital to investigate further, as he was going downhill quickly. I was at a function in the old Premiership stand with my teammates when I saw that I had missed a call from the hospital. I walked out of the function to call them straight back.

The vet said Olly wasn't responding to treatment. At this point, they had him on a ventilator, which was costing an exorbitant amount per day, but I would have paid anything to get him healthy. He had been through a lot with me; I couldn't imagine life without him.

I drove straight to Werribee.

'He's not going to make it. We've done everything we can for him, but it's no good,' the vet said.

Then, he presented the worst form I've ever had to fill out. A consent form for Olly to be put down. He asked me if I wanted to be with him when it happened and, of course, I said yes. Now, anyone who has gone through this will know just how distressing it is.

When I went into the room to see Olly, he was in a bad way. He couldn't move. I could see his tail twitching as he tried to wag it because he was happy to see me. That broke my heart.

He was lying on a bench in a room full of computers, special equipment and other vets. None of them looked over. I suppose they wanted to give us that time and at least make us feel like we weren't being watched. I'm sure they've had to get used to seeing animals euthanised. I don't know how they do that job.

Olly went off peacefully, but I found it horrific. I still have his ashes and I'm going to keep them until I'm sure I'm living in my 'forever home'. (It is not easy to decide where that should be when your family live thousands of miles away and you love where you live.)

They did an autopsy on Olly, and it turned out he had been bitten by a snake. They thought it was a rare disease called degenerative myelopathy (comparable to ALS in humans), but, no, it turned out he was another Australian snake victim. The result of this autopsy upset me, because if I had known sooner that he had been bitten by a snake, I wouldn't have spent so long trying to save him. If you don't get your pet to a vet straight after they've been bitten, there's virtually no chance they'll survive.

Instead, all I succeeded in doing was prolonging his suffering. I still feel horrible about it. Olly had been lying in a vet's office for a week, wondering why I had handed him over to a stranger. His attempted recovery took one week and cost $8,000. All to no avail.

It's fair to say that, growing up, I never thought I'd have a family pet killed by a snake. I'm sure you know already, but St Patrick banished them all from Ireland. He was a tough bucko that St Paddy. Pity there were no flights to Australia at the time or he might have done the same here.

After Olly left us, I went out to the car to try to gather

myself. I started sobbing as soon as I heard Bec's voice on the phone and had to deliver the news. I called Dave Johnson, who was our player-development officer at the time. All of the players who had joined the club were due to get together for dinner. I just couldn't face it.

'No worries. Is everything okay?' he enquired.

'Yeah, fine,' I managed to say before I started blubbering again.

Dave offered me a day off but there was no way I was going to take it. I didn't care how I was feeling, I wasn't going to miss a session.

When I went back into the club the following day, I was determined to keep it together. But during an ankle-strapping session, one of our trainers – affectionately known as 'Frenchie' because he was, unsurprisingly, French (what an original nickname, I know) – asked me, 'How's Olly going?' He, of course, asked in that melodic French inflection that politely but urgently requests information.

I had to jump from the table and leave immediately for fear of bursting into tears again. I walked out and went for a walk to try to compose myself.

When I returned, I just said, 'Sorry, he got put down yesterday.'

I got through training but later that day, Simon Lloyd called. Simon, who was head of footy at the time and Matthew Lloyd's (Essendon club legend) brother, was worried when he heard about the ankle-strapping outpour.

'I heard about your dog, mate. Is everything okay?' he asked. 'You do know that it's okay to take a few days off if you want?'

I had joined the club. Again, I rejected the offer. But I really appreciated that they were willing to do that for me, and I also appreciated my teammates' reaction.

Tom 'Stewie' Stewart, who arrived at the club the same time as me and has since become one of my closest friends, was one of the first players to come up to check I was okay. It was a small gesture but one that meant a lot at the time. I could tell pretty early on that we were going to get on great. Over the years since then, we've shared a lot.

Not long after I joined Geelong, I became a dad for the second time, and Stewie became a dad for the first time. We have shared some great conversations about all things parenting. The good and the bad.

When Flynn was born, the Carlton group was really young. Nobody in my circle of friends at the time had kids, so I never had anybody to talk with. Sometimes, parents just need someone to vent to – to find out that what you're going through isn't unusual. At the Cats, there are plenty of dads, and Stewie and I spent many a day talking about our kids in the locker room. I really valued those chats, and I think he did too.

Another friendly face in the change room was Mark O'Connor. Mark was an extremely talented Gaelic footballer from Kerry, who the Cats had signed in the off-season. I was pleased to have a compatriot in the change room again, and I loved how the club was embracing the Irish experiment. Mark is seven years younger than me, and I liked having the opportunity to pay forward what the Ó hAilpíns had done for me. They had really looked after me in my early years, and I was determined to do the same for him.

When it came to settling into the new regime, no one was more helpful than Hendo. We had arrived at Carlton at the same time, so I had spent my entire career with him as a teammate, with the exception of the 2016 season when he left the Blues. I was still getting over how things had been at Carlton and especially with Bolts and, as Hendo had already navigated the transition, his help was invaluable.

I always sat next to him in the meeting room. After one meeting, which went on for 20 minutes maximum, Chris Scott apologised for how long it had dragged on. *Is he joking? Does he think that was a long meeting?* Some of our meetings at the Blues had gone on so long I'd started to think the coaches were getting paid by the hour.

I was sitting there in shock when Lachie nudged me and laughed.

'He's serious. That was a long meeting,' he said with a wide smile.

Meetings weren't only shorter at the Cats, there was a very different tone. While Bolts was more 'here's the plan, do it my way or you're gone', Scotty was all about 'this is how I think we should play, what do you think?' And when he asked what you thought, he actually meant it. He listened and took everything on board. He was much more of a conversationalist.

To him, a short meeting was a good meeting, and there were a lot fewer of them too. At Carlton, we had to do these bullshit leadership-development meetings where I felt like I learned absolutely nothing. They always felt like an appointment in your calendar that justified the hiring of some consultancy group. There were none of those meetings at Geelong – just real leaders. Most importantly, Scott was always measured and rational. Whether you'd won 10 games in a row or lost 10, his tone never differed.

Paddy Dangerfield had heard Hendo and me discussing the meeting duration and was laughing too. You might not expect to hear this, but the guy is extremely laid back. You don't envisage someone as credentialled and respected as him to be that chilled out. But he is. He's just perfect for Geelong.

I made my debut for the club in round one in 2017, along with Stewie. We played Fremantle over in Perth, and I managed to kick my first goal for the club as the siren sounded at the end of the first half. All of the boys got around me as we walked off the field.

It was great to have that box ticked. I was glad it had happened early so it didn't become 'a thing'. The feeling was just as special as when I kicked my first goal in AFL. And as debuts go, this was far superior to my first match for the Blues when the Sherrin had bounced over my head.

As soon as I kicked it, I knew it was going through, and evidently so did Lincoln McCarthy. When I watched the replay back, I saw that he put his hands up in the air as soon as I kicked the ball and sprinted straight towards me. Harry Taylor had passed the ball to me, and he was the first one in to celebrate.

Geelong is a team that really celebrates new players. They know how to embrace you and get the best out of you. At the end of the match, as we walked off the field, Joel Selwood put his arm around me. I officially felt like a Geelong player.

That year, we won the first five games of the season before hitting a form slump. We lost to Collingwood, the Gold Coast Suns and then Essendon. As I walked down the race and into the rooms after our round-eight loss to the Bombers, I was expecting a major bake from Scotty. I hadn't had one yet and, surely, now we were at round eight and had lost three in a row, it was time.

We don't always have meetings after matches, as Scotty likes to be calm when he delivers his message to the team. He says he never wants to say anything in the heat of the moment that he may regret. But on this particular day, we were told to assemble in the meeting room.

'Here we go,' I thought as I fastened my seatbelt, Johnny Barker style.

Much to my surprise, when Scotty walked into the room, he was calm.

'What do you think we can do better, boys?' he asked. 'If there's something we can change about our weekly schedule, to prepare better, let us know. We'll look at it.'

That was it. That was the meeting.

Hang on, this wasn't right. Was he actually treating us like adults? Was he really asking for our input? Not for the first time I asked myself, *Is this a trick? If we provide feedback, will he bake us then?* But no, that wasn't Scotty's style. He genuinely wanted to know what we could do to be better. He gave us ownership of it and some responsibility to help him fix it.

We did our match review and, again, he was completely measured. In all of my time at the club, not once has the coaching team shown video footage of a player messing up, just for the sake of it. Guys don't get singled out and made to feel bad about themselves. They just don't.

That week at training, the intensity lifted. Not only did we beat the Western Bulldogs, the reigning Premiers, by 23 points in our next match, but we also laid 134 tackles. Scotty's calm response had elicited a fierce response in us, which saw us rebound in a week from a pathetic effort, where we laid only 40 tackles, to breaking the club record for tackles. No shouting or roaring or banging on tables, but 94 more tackles than a week earlier.

Next, we beat Port Adelaide, before making it three in a

row with a 22-point win over the eventual Grand Finalists, the Adelaide Crows. We only lost three more games for the remainder of the season and finished second on the ladder.

I've never hidden my motivation for going to Geelong. It was all about achieving success. In my first season, when we finished second on the ladder, you'd think that I would have been celebrating such a feat. That the contrast with where I had come from would be so stark that it would feel momentous. But it didn't. There's just something about Geelong that makes winning feel ordinary, like a habit. And they bring you into that vortex straightaway. There was no fanfare. We hadn't won a Premiership. We had just finished second on the ladder.

We lost our qualifying final to the eventual champions Richmond by 51 points, but with the double chance, we had the opportunity to make up for it a week later. We did, smashing the Sydney Swans by 59 points in the semi-final. If you're reading this in Ireland, you're thinking that if we won a semi-final, that means we were into the final? I'm afraid not. A semi-final only gets you into a 'preliminary final' – I know, I don't get it either.

While the finals system still doesn't make sense to me, preliminary finals certainly do. Unfortunately, I've lost a few so I'm well aware of what match comes next if you win, and what you're missing out on if you don't.

Anyway, our semi-final win over the Swans had secured our spot in the preliminary final against the Adelaide Crows. It was my first opportunity to play in that stage of the competition. The preliminary final is the penultimate match before the AFL Grand Final – win and you're in, lose and you miss out on one of the biggest days in the Australian sports calendar. I should know.

Preliminary-final losses are the worst kind of losses, and I was about to experience my first. Back then, it felt like the worst defeat I had suffered in my career but, reflecting on it now, that game isn't even in my top three worst losses.

I don't know what was more disappointing, the fact we lost or the fact that the Adelaide Crows beat us after doing the now infamous 'Power Stance'. The club had decided to adopt this pose during the anthem before each of their finals in the 2017 season. I'll try to describe it, although it's not easy to put into words. Please know I'm cringing as I write.

They were standing there, legs splayed, arms thrust down, muscles flexed, as if they were superheroes – instead of respectfully standing with their arms down by their sides (which in my view, they should have been during the national anthem). Just google it, it's bloody embarrassing.

The 'Power Stance' didn't feel very powerful to me. At best, I was bemused and thought it quite comical. At worst, it was cringeworthy. A couple of Crows players have since admitted they felt the same.

After performing the 'Power Stance' they beat us by 61 points at Adelaide Oval that day. They were favourites to win the flag, but it didn't work out that way. Richmond clearly didn't enjoy their up-close performance of the 'Power Stance' and, despite being underdogs, belted them by 48 points in a very one-sided Grand Final a week later. It ended up being the start of a pretty bleak period for the Crows, while the Tigers went on to create a dynasty – three Premierships in four years.

In the off-season, Geelong was at the centre of one of the biggest trade deals in the history of the AFL. Gary Ablett Junior, the beloved two-time Premiership player and club legend, wanted to come home, and struck a deal to leave the Gold Coast Suns. It was big news at the club, in Geelong and across the AFL community.

When Junior first arrived back at the club, his second coming, he had that special aura about him; just like Mick Malthouse had when I first saw him. Being the son of a club legend, Gary Ablett Senior, and having two Brownlow medals to your own name as well as eight All-Australians will do that for you.

I'd seen him on the football field when he played for the Suns, of course. But sharing a change room and being his locker-room buddy was next level. Because I played in the number 2 and he played in the number 4 jumper, we were right next to each other.

We were locker buddies – but he didn't spend much time

at his. He was usually playing basketball on a small court we had out the back. He spent so much time out there shooting hoops. He played with an air about him that suggested he believed his basketball skills were on the same level as his AFL skills. Which of course would be impossible!

I'm not sure if he ever noticed what I chose to display in my locker: AFL footy cards. You read that right – I collect them. I used to display my teammates' footy cards in my locker. But before I did, I would get them to sign them. I loved it when I found a footy card with a teammate wearing their old club colours. For example, my Gary Rohan card showed him in his Sydney Swans colours. Other big-name footy cards in the number 2 locker included Matthew Scarlett, Joel Selwood, Paddy Dangerfield and, of course, my best friend, Tom Stewart. I didn't have to buy these footy cards: fans would give us their spares, and I think they found it quite comical that I collected my teammates' cards, just like they did.

As it happens, I didn't have a footy card of Junior – only because I collected them as I came across them. His would be a highly coveted card to have.

Junior, also known as Gaz, was open, approachable and warm from the start. He's a big softie. And, in tune with the Geelong way, he was always up for a laugh. At training, I watched him up close and he oozed talent (major understatement warning). His skills were silky smooth and every possession was clean. He was a little bit magic. I was always aware that I was in the presence of greatness when he was around.

He wasn't at the peak of his powers when he came back to the club, but there were flashes of genius every now and then.

Our Easter Monday round-two clash with Hawthorn in 2018 stands out for a couple of reasons. It was his second game after what was dubbed the 'return of the prodigal son' and the first time the 'holy trinity' of midfielders had played together – Ablett, Patrick Dangerfield and Joel Selwood all on the field at the same time. We lost by a point in one of the games of the season, but Gary provided a major match highlight. He took a huge mark, and it was one of those times where, even as a teammate, you have to just stand back and admire what you're seeing. It's like a bucket-list fan moment that you can't miss, but you've quickly got to get back to work. He notched up 35 possessions that day, but ended up on the losing side in a thriller.

Despite Gary's return, our 2018 season was an anomaly. We only finished eighth on the ladder, scraping into finals before going on to lose an elimination final to the Melbourne Demons. It's always disappointing to lose a final but it hurt more as we had beaten them in both our regular-season fixtures. In fairness, we had only won by three- (round one) and two-point (round 18) margins – so they just managed to make it third time lucky.

One of those three matches with the Demons resulted in a

major career highlight. I got to experience every AFL player's childhood dream – kicking a goal after the siren to win the game. We were 23 points down going into the last quarter when Matthew Scarlett, our defensive coach, tapped me on the shoulder and told me to jump in with the forward group for their three-quarter-time address. In my entire career up to that point, I hadn't played a second in the forward line, so this was as much of a shock to me as it was to the rest of the playing group. Matthew had joked about me having the potential to be a good forward. He'd mentioned my size and strength, and the fact I was a good kick in training, but I thought it was always tongue-in-cheek. Turned out, he wasn't joking. It was happening.

I did what I was told and trundled off to the forwards to find out what the plan was for the last quarter. You'd think that having played in defence for as long as I have, I'd know how to be a forward. This was not the case. All I knew was what I didn't like forwards doing to me when I was on them, so I decided to do that. I hated when they would loop around me and keep running, looking for blocks, never staying still. It frustrated me. At least I knew it was a tactic that could work. I barely listened to the huddle; I was too busy thinking about this unexpected change of position.

The Demons kicked the first goal of the final term to drag the margin out to 29 points but then we took control, winning clearance after clearance. We peppered their defence.

It was Tom Hawkins' thirtieth birthday and he celebrated in style. He kicked four goals in the final quarter and seven for the night. Who needs birthday cake when you can do that instead? I've seen him do this countless times, but I always appreciate the opportunity to watch one of the all-time greats go to work.

I managed to kick a goal midway through the last quarter and was getting my hands on the footy. But, with 30 seconds left on the clock, the ball was locked in our defensive 50 metres. It was frenetic and with players desperately diving on the ball, it seemed virtually impossible for us to go end to end.

With 25 seconds to go, Junior managed to slip a handball out to Stewie, who kicked it to Daniel Menzel on the wing. His kick found Hawk, who marked it and quickly handballed it to Mitch Duncan on the overlap, who kicked it long inside the forward 50. I managed to lose my opponent and mark it.

I still remember lying on the ground knowing full well that there couldn't be much more than a few seconds left. Before I could stand up, the siren went.

We were trailing by four points. The match was literally on my boot.

I'd gone from never playing in the forward line to having a kick after the siren to win the match. As I stood there, lining up my shot while Melbourne players jumped up and waved their arms in front of me, remarkably, I felt no nerves. Just excitement. The prospect of missing genuinely never entered my mind.

In fact, this was a free hit in a way. It had seemed impossible for us to come back when we were 29 points down and even more so when the footy was locked in our back half with seconds to play.

But here we were. I'd already kicked one goal. Surely, I could add another?

I did. And I've never celebrated a goal harder. It was pandemonium. As the Dees stood back in shock, I was swamped by teammates jumping over the top of each other to get to me. A goal after the siren is as good as it gets. One of the highlights of my career. Now, I'm not saying I'm a hero, you know, but I'm also not saying I'm not a hero.

I've mentioned how bad Mammy is at watching matches, especially if they're close. Up in the stand that night, Bec called her to find out what she thought of my goal after the siren. She had been pacing up and down in the backyard and hadn't even seen it. She eventually did on the highlights. For a woman who hates watching me play live, she's a great one to watch highlights on repeat. She loves watching football, as long as she knows it's a favourable result for me.

I said that we 'scraped into finals' (technically that's true as we finished eighth) but when I reminisce, it was a relatively impressive end to the year. I broke my hand in round 21 against Hawthorn and played the rest of the season with it strapped. I didn't even know it had happened until, full of adrenaline, I looked down at it and noticed that one of my knuckles was about an inch away from where it should be. I'm no doctor but I knew that wasn't ideal. It wasn't too painful, so I entered another contest to spoil and let's just say the impact definitely didn't help.

After the match, it was fat and swollen. I think they call it a 'boxer's fracture'. That isn't an official medical term, but I believe it's one of the less severe ways to break your hand, and it ended up being one of the least inhibiting setbacks I've endured.

In round 22, we absolutely blitzed Fremantle. They were winning at quarter-time, and we kicked the next 23 goals to win the match. They were 3.2.20 at quarter-time and they finished the match 3.7.25. We were 1.5.11 after the first term and finished 24.14.158. Tom Hawkins kicked six goals that day, and my broken hand and I chipped in with two. Our 23 unanswered goals are an AFL/VFL record to this day. The 133-point defeat was the biggest losing margin in Fremantle's history back then.

A week later, we pumped Gary Ablett's old club, the Gold Coast Suns, by 102 points to secure our spot in the finals. Melbourne hadn't played in finals since 2006, and it goes without saying that we were a much more experienced side, but they defeated us by 29 points at the MCG. No goals after the siren in that one.

The year 2019 began strangely. I missed the first five rounds of the season due to a knee injury.

I'd had a great run injury wise. I missed the last match of the season in 2012 but, since round one in 2013, I'd played every match for Carlton and then Geelong. My knee put an end to that streak. But there was an upside to the timing of that: Bec and I were expecting a new addition to our family, so I was around a lot more to help.

On 4 April, the Cats were playing the Adelaide Crows in Adelaide in round three. Bec was a week overdue. I was still injured, but planning to watch that evening.

Very early in the morning, Bec's waters broke and we went to hospital. They wanted to move things on, so she was induced. It was at this point, Bec claims, I joked, 'This isn't going to take too long, is it? It would be great to watch the footy tonight.' I don't remember this, so surely not. But Bec insisted it should go in the book.

When they started inducing Bec, I went outside to move my car. By the time I came back, she was in full-blown labour. Turned out I was right: we would end up watching the football.

Our second son, Rafferty, joined us at 10.30 a.m. Later that evening, I posted a message on the team WhatsApp congratulating the boys on a 24-point win, which I had watched with my new son in my arms. He had turned up in plenty of time to watch that Adelaide Oval win.

Yet again, as Bec's labour had moved so quickly, there was no time for medication. If you're counting, you'll know that I've had three epidurals and Bec has had zero. In another unsubstantiated claim made by her, she says I was joking that her screams of pain were putting everyone in the waiting room off giving birth. Surely not.

The year 2019 was a good year. The club won its first Minor Premiership since 2008. Quick explainer for Irish readers – the Minor Premiership means you've finished the regular home-and-away season on top of the ladder. To make the finals series, you need to finish in the top eight. If you didn't know we'd finished top, you wouldn't be able to tell. Finishing first place doesn't matter at Geelong. There was no hoopla, that's for sure. Only Premierships matter at the Cattery.

Don't get me wrong, finishing top two is also important – so you get a double chance and a home final. Not that we ever get the latter, but I'll have a rant about that one later.

Actually! Let me rant about that one now. Geelong doesn't necessarily get to play their 'home games' at home. For those reading in Ireland and not aware, we have a beautiful home stadium called GMHBA (also referred to locally as Kardinia Park – GMHBA is the health insurance company who sponsor us), which has a capacity of 40,000. But when there's a blockbuster game in the regular season or it's a final where a big attendance is expected, our 'home' matches that we've worked hard to earn when it comes to the finals series get taken away from us and are staged at the MCG with its 100,000 capacity.

For example, if we finish first and earn a home final in the first week of finals against, say, Richmond who hypothetically finished fourth, we would be forced to play our home fixture at Richmond's home ground – the MCG. Does that seem fair to you?

Anyway, let's move it on with the warning that Cats fans (and I will always be a Cats man) can, will and do have the right to go on a tangent about why we don't ever get home advantage in a final, at any time, and without warning. It's indefensible and it's bullshit, but it's a money decision.

But, for now, let's get back to 2019.

After finishing top of the ladder, we made it as far as the preliminary final against Richmond. The Tigers were at their peak. Think Dusty Martin, Trent Cotchin, Jack Riewoldt, Tom Lynch and co. Despite all that talent, we were 21 points up at half-time. We thought we were going to pull off a major upset.

We didn't. They ended up winning by 19 points. I mention their star players but the most impressive aspect of that Richmond side, and the reason they beat us, was they were a champion team, not a team of champions. Their system was elite. They were just highly functioning and moved the ball quickly and effortlessly. It was impressive to watch, although not when you were playing against them.

The thing I admired most about them was that, even when they started winning Premierships, they never got arrogant or lippy. I respect that. I liked them as much as I could like an opposition team.

This prelim loss felt even worse than 2017. Losing a prelim is always bad, but you start to feel the cumulative effect of lost opportunities.

A year later, I was going to find out that preliminary final losses are even worse than Grand Final losses. And, yes, it's a shame I even have that comparison in my repertoire.

CHAPTER 8

Playing in Exile

2020 WAS, AS THE AFL DESCRIBED IT, 'A YEAR LIKE no other'.

That's the phrase they used when the league was shut down because of Covid. That phrase was regurgitated ad nauseam, even after the competition was back up and running, and other codes started to run with it too.

Before everything went pear-shaped and I had to leave Victoria, during the time when restaurants were still open and we could wine and dine as we pleased, I took Bec for what I told her would be a birthday celebration at Crown Hotel in Melbourne. It was 1 February.

It was a dinner I had been organising for a while. I was planning to bring a ring.

I was going to propose and Bec had no idea, thanks to the club's help. I didn't know how to pay for a ring without my future wife noticing a large sum of money disappearing from our account, so I'd asked for their expertise.

The club had helped with this conundrum before. When I'd found the ring I wanted the club paid for it and organised to take the cost out of my wage in instalments. Perfect. Bec would be none the wiser. That's as long as I managed to get it to the hotel without her noticing.

When we arrived and dropped our bags in the room, I pretended to have forgotten my jacket in the car park. I told Bec I should go down and grab it, in case we left the hotel later. I went downstairs to retrieve it. I had carefully tucked the precious ring away in a pocket.

When I returned, I asked the big question.

She said 'yes' – straightaway, of course – how could she not? I am, after all, the world's sexiest man.

If you've been reading attentively up until now, you'll know that she has been head over heels for me since day one. How could she not be? I'm extremely lovable. And she loved the ring, which I had picked all by myself.

Phew, I thought. I'm not sure how the club would have dealt with that refund.

Our friends who came along to meet us, thinking it was a surprise birthday dinner, were delighted to hear our news.

Guests of honour were, you guessed it, my good friend Levi Casboult and his wife Hayley. They had introduced us, after all. Levi turned up with a bottle of 1989 Grange, a gift for my thirtieth birthday. From CQ nightclub to a civilised dinner – with no apricot chicken in sight – and high-end wine. Look how far we'd come. And I mean Levi and me, not Bec and me.

I had confided in two people about the proposal. At Christmastime, when we were visiting Bec's parents, I approached her dad, Rob, while he was pottering around the garage. It was awkward, as he could see me looking at him, sizing him up in a way that indicated I had something to tell him. Unsure of exactly how to start the conversation, I went in for some small talk before I eventually informed him of my intentions.

'I just want you to know that I'm going to ask Bec to marry me. I don't know exactly when, but soon, and because I'm not sure when I'll see you again, I wanted to take this opportunity to tell you.'

I reassured him how much I loved her and that I would continue doing whatever I could to make sure Bec, Flynn and Rafferty would be looked after and provided for. I hope Rob already knew that, but it seemed appropriate to remind him.

Then, he did something that surprised me. He started crying and hugged me. 'I'm so proud of you, and her – of the parents you are.'

When Rob recovered, we went to find Bec's mum, Deb. She was delighted. I'm so glad I got to tell them in person. I wasn't to know then, but with the way the year went, that soon couldn't be taken for granted.

Our season began in March with a 32-point defeat to Greater Western Sydney, behind closed doors at Giants Stadium. Just days later, the competition was suspended. When it finally resumed in June, we only played four matches in Melbourne.

When we walked off the field after our round-five win against the Gold Coast Suns, we were told to go home and pack our bags. We would be leaving Victoria the following morning for a hub in Queensland. That was it, just 12 hours' notice. The AFL was racing the clock as the Victorian government was expected to close the state border. If we didn't get out before that happened, we wouldn't get out at all, and there'd be no chance of the competition continuing.

When I look back on it – and who wants to look back on that time at all? – I'm glad we didn't know how long we would be away for. The AFL assured us it would be a maximum of 31 days. It ended up being 115.

If you couldn't organise family to get together and leave immediately, then you had to go without them. There would be opportunities for them to join, but the players had to fly to the Gold Coast the following morning.

At the time, the league was saying clubs needed to be 'agile' and the fixtures would be 'fluid'. It should have been more obvious to us that they were preparing us for constant uncertainty, but no one had ever been through this before.

Bec is very independent, and Flynn was starting prep school, so they were happy to stay back. After all, it was only for a month. That month turned into eleven weeks – which, again, I'm glad I didn't know at the time. It would have been a tough goodbye.

Before I go on, I'd like to clarify something.

My overall experience in the hub was a positive one. For the most part, we had it pretty bloody good. It presented plenty of challenges, but just know that when I mention some of the hard times, I'm fully aware that we had it better than the vast majority of society at the time. This was a time when people were losing their jobs, left, right and centre. When families all over Australia were trying desperately to pay their bills and keep food on the table.

With that rather substantial caveat in place, let me describe our lockdown experience. We were staying at the Southport Sharks Mantra Hotel. We had the place to ourselves and, because our team is so tight knit, it was really good fun. The fact we were playing well helped too.

I did have to endure 11 weeks without Bec and the lads and, by the end of it, I was just about ready to crack. I'd had enough and was something of a zombie day to day, waiting for them to arrive. It really began to weigh me down to the point where I didn't want to be around any of my teammates outside of training. I would take one of the rental cars we had on site (again we had it good, I know) and drive around for an hour or two, just to be alone.

Knowing my parents had it tough back home was an added worry. Daddy's Parkinson's meant that he was high risk, so they had to be really careful to ensure he didn't get sick.

As tough as my 2020 season was, it didn't compare to that of my compatriot Conor McKenna. Conor was playing with Essendon at the time and, in June, he tested positive for Covid-19. He was treated like AFL patient zero.

With his test result threatening to derail the season (important to note it didn't – in fact, only one other player he had contact with had to quarantine, and that player never tested positive), the media in that moment demonstrated the dark side of Melbourne's AFL obsession. There was rampant speculation about how he might have contracted it, and one TV channel even analysed 'exclusive' footage of him blowing his nose at training. It was insane, by any standards. Conor ended up retiring from AFL that September and there's no doubt that the way he was treated contributed heavily to that. He has since returned to Australia and played in the Brisbane Lions' AFL Grand Final loss to Collingwood in 2023.

Round 14 provided an unwelcome distraction, and brought about the most painful injury I've sustained in my career. Forget back injuries, knee injuries and epidurals, this incident made all of that seem minor.

We were playing the Western Bulldogs and we ended up winning by 11 points – no thanks to me. Let's say I was a little bit off after an incident in the second quarter.

After a collision with Jackson Macrae, I could barely breathe. Former Hawthorn legend Luke Hodge was commentating on TV from the boundary and said in the coverage that I was making a sound he 'had never heard on a football field before'. Unfortunately, this was true. I was in agony. It was hell to breathe out – like nails were prodding my lungs during the exhale – and the sound of that process was concerning.

But, of course, I played on. That makes sense, right? As I've said, I have a mentality that you play unless you physically can't. Technically, I was physically able to play, despite my inability to breathe normally. As far as I was concerned, enough air was getting in for me to continue.

When I returned to the field, I copped more knocks and even a cut above my eyebrow that needed stitching up. That took my mind off my breathing problems for a while! Despite my physical situation, I was upset at how badly I was playing and at one point threw my mouthguard on the boundary in frustration.

After the match, I found out I had played with broken ribs. That explained that awful sound. I hope I never hear it again.

When Bec and the boys eventually arrived in Queensland, they had to do two weeks of quarantine on the Gold Coast with other families who had travelled. My trio were in the last group to arrive. They left Victoria on 1 September.

Because of this compulsory quarantine, Bec and the lads ended up missing my 200th-game milestone. They watched from quarantine, and we lost to Richmond. No family there to see it, and a loss at Metricon Stadium was not how I imagined my 200th match. I was chaired off the field and, if you look back at the pictures of that day, I look miserable. We all looked miserable.

As you may already know, the pictures of my 250th milestone are a big contrast to that. I'm very happy there's one on the front of this book!

Anyway, back to 2020 for now.

The Cattery on tour on the Gold Coast was a harmonious group. While we were well looked after, it was still challenging for parents to persist with homeschooling in that environment, which is probably what the kids loved – it was basically a massive holiday for them. Flynn and Rafferty thought it was a big adventure.

They loved hanging out with other players' kids, and it was like a little community where everyone looked out for each other. Fortunately, lots of Cats players had children, so there were plenty of parents helping each other out, and plenty of friends for the kids to play with. All the while, children in Victoria were in lockdown, while our kids maintained a social connection with their peers, and we know how lucky they were to do that.

My best memories of the hub are of the rooftop bar. This became our pseudo meeting room post-game, and we would go up there for drinks. Many a nice bottle of red was consumed there.

You get the picture; we had it really good compared to most people.

So, you can imagine what we thought when players from other Victorian clubs started going on TV and whinging about their situation, about 'how tough' they had it.

I was horrified. How low does your emotional intelligence have to be to do a live interview, broadcast into Victoria, where people are locked in their houses, as their livelihoods and businesses implode, and whinge about your life in a beachside holiday resort? Jesus wept. It was the ultimate demonstration of entitlement, and it gave the AFL playing group as a whole a bad name.

Don't get me wrong, when you put every player and staff member and their partners and families into one hotel, there are dynamics that need to be navigated, but the Cats were happy hubbers for the most part.

I should at this point take the time to say how grateful I am to Bec, who not only stayed back with the kids and did a lot of homeschooling on her own before travelling to Queensland, but settled right in when she arrived, rolling with the new routine and making sure the boys did too. Bec got along with everyone and never complained. I know how lucky I am in this way.

As a group, we were happy on the field as well as off the field. We finished fourth on the ladder and, while we had a poor start to finals, losing our qualifying final to Port Adelaide, we hammered both Collingwood and the Brisbane Lions to book our spot in the Grand Final against Richmond. I was particularly pleased with our 40-point win over the Brisbane Lions, as they had managed to have a pretty 'normal' year, living at home, while we had to uproot our whole lives to stay in the competition. I was proud that the group was so tight; it had worked to our advantage.

Making it to my first Grand Final was strange for a few reasons. One was that we'd had a big win in the preliminary final, the match was over well before the final siren. I kicked a goal in the fourth quarter that felt as though it had put the result beyond doubt and, when the siren sounded and the big dance was booked, it was a slightly surreal feeling. I couldn't believe it. It wasn't at all how I imagined making my first Grand Final – gearing up to play it in a hub in Queensland, and not at the MCG.

Even the date was weird. I had dreamed of making it to the last Saturday in September my whole career, but because the season had been suspended, the Grand Final was scheduled for 24 October at the Gabba in Brisbane. The Lions must have been gutted. It was an unexpected chance to stage a home final, and they missed out. Hopefully, for many reasons, that won't happen again for a while.

The shared accommodation situation meant the Grand Final build-up was unique. If we had been in Melbourne, both teams would have been doing a Grand Final parade together. It's traditional on the day before the match for teams to parade through the city centre and wave to thousands of fans lining the streets, before a photo shoot with the trophy and the final coaches' and captains' press conferences.

But because we were in a hub, both teams were sharing a hotel. Players with families were grouped in the same accommodation, so, in the build-up, you'd be sharing facilities with the likes of Richmond Premiership player Jack Riewoldt and his kids. You'd think that would feel weird, but it actually didn't. I don't know why. Maybe because everything was so strange, nothing felt strange anymore.

Jack became one of my favourite players before he retired, but it wasn't always the case. Over the course of my career, there have been players I've taken an instantaneous and irrational dislike to. Not because of anything they've done in particular but, rather, because of my preconceived notions of what they might be like. Jack was one such player. He had an air of confidence that rubbed me up the wrong way.

As discussed, I'd been devastated by our loss to Richmond in the 2019 prelim. After the siren went and Richmond had secured their spot in the Grand Final, instead of celebrating the victory, Jack came straight over and offered words of consolation.

What a class act. Immediately, it changed my opinion of him. This was not the first or last time I would be forced to reassess my first judgement of a player. I think part of me likes to dislike the opposition and create an 'us or them' mentality. Generally, though, when I meet these players I hold in disdain, they're really nice. They're not the bad guy and/or complete tool I've built them up to be in my mind. And as much as I sometimes resist, I end up really liking them. Which is annoying.

Even though it was Grand Final week, I was desperate to win a Premiership medallion and Jack was trying to prevent that from happening. I liked bumping into him at the hotel. I did, and I still have, enormous respect for him. What fans may or may not find surprising is that, away from the football field, we are all very cordial with each other. It was nice to meet other players in a different environment.

Watching the second preliminary final after we had booked our place in the Grand Final, I felt confident we could beat either team but, truthfully, I was hoping Port Adelaide would win. I really thought we would beat them in a decider, despite the fact we'd lost to them in the qualifying final. They had only won by 16 points, but I felt like we had their measure.

Richmond had won two out of the previous three flags. They were clinical, and they were after a third Premiership. They wanted to create a dynasty, and we were the only thing standing in their way.

Having said that, I thought we could beat them too. That's the Geelong way – we always think we can win. I don't remember a time that I didn't think we would beat the opposition.

The enormity of the occasion first dawned on me when I saw my jumper. There it was, written on the front: 2020 Grand Final. It was real.

The loss felt just as real. The Tigers defeated us by 31 points. They were the better team on the night.

When the siren went, Jack Riewoldt did it again. Instead of going to celebrate his third Premiership with his teammates, he walked over to console me. It was the chat I never wanted to have with him again, but I was blown away by the gesture. At that point, I didn't know if it would ever happen for me, but I struggled to imagine that, if it did, I would have the time to offer words of consolation to my opponent. What a class act Jack Riewoldt is.

When we went back to the hotel after the match, it felt like a wake. We had had so many fun nights during the year, but this wasn't going to be one of them. As we got off the bus, a young employee who had looked after us during our stay was trying to cheer us up by handing out beers on arrival. He was met with thunderous faces. He had not seen us this way before. We assembled in a function room to drown our sorrows.

At one point in the evening, Rhys Stanley and I went up to the hotel rooftop, accompanied by two bottles of our favourite red wine. By the end of the night, a few more had joined, including Tom Stewart. The rooftop banter ended on a good note. I woke up with a hangover, but I still believed that we were capable of winning the Grand Final. It *would* happen for us, eventually.

You'd think a Grand Final loss would be the worst loss of your career, right? But it would soon become a distant second to what happened in 2021.

I've explained my irrational disdain for certain players I haven't even met off the field. Well, sometimes, it extends to squads. There are whole teams that, to put it mildly, I'm not keen on. One of those teams is the Brisbane Lions. Not because of how they play – they're actually an excellent team to watch – but rather because of a specific incident that happened early in 2021.

The 2021 season was another year of disruption because of Covid. While it was more manageable because we were used to uncertainty and the situation was less severe, yet again it was punctuated by snap lockdowns, last-minute scheduling changes and, in some cases, reduced crowds.

The finals series, including the Grand Final, ended up being played interstate but during the regular home and away season, we were playing home fixtures in Geelong and we were very grateful for that.

We started the year by losing to the Adelaide Crows in Adelaide, and we were looking forward to hosting the Brisbane Lions in round two at GMHBA Stadium. Having beaten them in the preliminary final the year before, we thought it was a good chance to get back on track. In the end, it was a thriller and we won by a solitary point.

But that's not what I remember most about that match. At quarter-time, we were leading by 16 points, and things got a little feisty. Both sets of players got into a little tussle walking off the pitch. Words were being exchanged on both sides, but it was the words of Harris Andrews that would cement Brisbane's place on what I call my 'list of disdain'. As I walked up to our huddle, I could hear Andrews shouting. He was sledging us about our performance in the Grand Final. I'm pretty sure he used the word embarrassing – if not, it was something along those lines.

Now just to put this into context, we had beaten them, on their home deck, to make said Grand Final, in a year when we were in a hub, and they were living their normal lives.

Really, are you fucking kidding me? I know this might not seem like a big deal, and players talk shit to each other all the time, but this really rubbed me up the wrong way.

I was incredulous. I'll say it again – we had beaten them and beaten them well, on their home turf, in the preliminary final, and now we were in the process of beating them again. I know this might not seem like a big deal, and players talk shit to each other all the time, but this really rubbed me up the wrong way. If we were so embarrassing, how bad must they be?

In that moment, I branded him a massive fuckwit. Harsh, I know – by all accounts he's a belter of a bloke. I'd met Harris off-field prior to this, during a bush-fire fundraiser match we played right before Covid hit, and thought he was a perfect gent. A joy to be around, even. But this annoyed the shit out of me.

Now look, losing grand finals or prelims happens. I've lost plenty myself and I wear the fact that we make it to so many prelims and Grand Finals like a badge of honour, even if we don't end up winning them. Unless provoked, I would never use that as material to sledge opponents. However, Harris was happy to use our Grand Final heartache as a sledge.

I almost never instigate sledging with an opposition player, but I'm always happy to get involved if I deem it necessary. I feel the same about getting in a scrap on the field. I'm more than happy to start throwing my weight around if I feel one of my teammates needs help. I like and respect opposition players who do the same for their teammates, but starting blues (fights) for no reason or sledging about a Grand Final loss when you're playing badly? That's just fuckwittery.

I'll finish by saying I kicked two goals in that match, and we won but by just one point, which was extremely satisfying. As you can tell, I don't hold grudges at all.

Having said all that, Harris has since edged his way back onto the list of players I quite like. For one, he has a history of carrying on while standing the mark – which is something I have done and find very funny. But most importantly, he has played a significant role in helping another Irishman become a premiership player. In 2024, he led the Lions and Conor McKenna to Premiership glory. It's almost like I shouldn't judge people so harshly so quickly … nah, that can't be right. Sorry, Harris.

A hamstring injury late in the season meant I missed the last two rounds and our qualifying final loss to Port Adelaide. But I came straight back into the team for our semi-final against GWS and hit the ground running, playing one of the better games of my career.

Tom Hawkins kicked five goals, including three in the final quarter, to seal a 35-point win. It was a fitting celebration for Joel Selwood, who became the all-time club record holder for matches played with 333 under his belt. He was chaired off the field by Hawkins and the man whose record he broke – former teammate and then assistant coach, Corey Enright. It's fair to say a good night was had by all. We were into another prelim. This time, we'd face Melbourne.

Our preparation for that match was far from ideal. A virus went through the Perth hotel we were staying in, and half the team was sick going into the game. It completely knocked the stuffing out of us.

We've no idea how we managed to get the virus, but the running gag has been that a rather suspect-looking jacuzzi might have been the culprit. I'm not sure how strong the correlation between blokes who got in the jacuzzi and blokes who got sick actually was, but, at the time, the numbers felt directly proportionate and it was a good story. If you're going to get a virus in the playing group, why not label ground zero as the jacuzzi?

To say we were lacklustre is an understatement, and Melbourne capitalised. We were thrashed by a whopping 83 points – a defeat by the eventual 2021 Premiers we deserved.

This was, and I hope will always remain, the worse defeat of my life. I considered starting this book talking about this loss, such was its impact on me. Walking off the field, I was distraught. I thought, *This is it for me.* I genuinely questioned whether I could keep doing this to myself. Why keep going back to the well when you just end up devastated? Maybe it's time to retire.

When I went into the locker room, I punched a wall and let out a loud scream. The mood was sombre, and this was very out of character for me, so it caught my teammates off-guard. This wasn't the first time they'd seen me angry, but this particular outburst didn't blend well with the quiet stoicism everybody else was exhibiting.

Just as I walked away to collect myself, a drug tester approached. *Really? Of all days.* I feel awful about this, but I told him to get fucked.

In case you're wondering, you can't tell drug testers to get fucked. And they don't leave if you do. They still follow you around until you produce a urine sample. On this particular night, he had to follow me around for a while. I stormed off to a quiet room in the back of our changing area and told him in no uncertain terms that he couldn't come in. He did, of course, wait at the open door where he could keep an eye on me, as when you've been informed that you've been selected for a drug test, the tester must be able to see you at all times, until you've produced your sample.

After a while, when I'd cooled down, I apologised. The guy was just trying to do his job. He graciously accepted it. I was then taken to another waiting area where I stayed until I managed to produce a sample.

What's worse than failing to produce a urine sample while contemplating retirement? Sitting next to one of the players from the team that just thrashed you as he also tries to beat dehydration. In this case, it was Christian Salem. We exchanged pleasantries and, of course, I offered him my best wishes for the Grand Final as I sipped on warm water (it's supposed to go 'through you' quicker). What a fucking nightmare. Can I please just have a piss and go home to bed?

By the time I was ready to go, the team bus had long since left. I was brought back to the hotel by Mark Worthington, who had waited until I was ready. Wortho was one of our player-welfare managers and is among the best people I've ever met in footy. He would do anything for you – he's an absolute gent. Unfortunately for him, I was in a horrible mood and made for terrible company on the drive back.

In that moment, if I had been given a choice, I would have retired. My inner monologue ran something like: *I can't keep doing this, I just can't. I can't keep getting this close and failing. It's time to stop. It's not worth it. It's killing me.*

The older you get, the worse the losses get. You're so aware that your chances are diminishing, and your football mortality starts to creep in and invade your thought process, particularly after bad losses. I've never felt it more acutely than I did that night.

When I walked into the hotel, the boys were having a few beers with their food. Now, I love to socialise, but on this occasion I was not feeling it. The sound of people laughing was infuriating to me.

For the record, I was in the wrong here. But I couldn't see it then, as I was ropable (furious). I stormed off to my room where I could fester alone in self-pity. Getting to sleep wasn't easy. I was still simmering, and downstairs was getting rowdier and rowdier as the evening went on.

The boys stayed up until 6 a.m., debriefing the season and drinking, which was a far healthier approach than the one

I chose, but I just didn't have it in me to pretend everything was okay – it wasn't.

I woke up the next morning and felt remorseful. I had clearly missed a good night so I could have a tanty (Irish readers should know that 'tanty' is slang for 'tantrum' – feel free to use this). I looked at my hungover teammates at breakfast and knew two things instantly – I'd missed a great night and I'd overreacted.

There was a cleanout in the coaching department in the off-season. Corey Enright (forward coach), Matthew Scarlett (defensive coach) and Matthew Knights (midfield coach) all left.

Former Cat James Kelly joined the coaching staff and he's worked with the backs ever since. James is one of the best coaches I've ever been lucky enough to work with. He is unbelievable. His people skills are elite; you just want to be around him. He's also a top-notch communicator. The way he delivers a message resonates with me. I can relate to his journey (he left Geelong to go to Essendon at the end of his playing career) and him guiding me through mine since 2021 has been a game-changer, literally.

We had a good start to 2022 despite losing a couple of games.

We lost to Sydney in round two, but that match at the Sydney Cricket Ground (SCG) was a circus. A very historic circus, mind you. Lance 'Buddy' Franklin kicked his 1,000th goal and fans stormed the ground. Looking back on it, I feel lucky to have been there to witness a piece of AFL folklore, but at the time I was filthy (angry). One minute you're playing a professional game of football and the next it feels you've involuntarily entered a mosh pit at a heavy-metal concert but you've been tasked with getting out as quickly as you can. Mayhem ensued.

There were guys running onto the pitch who were making a beeline for players. They didn't want a selfie with Buddy, they wanted to tell their mates in the pub they'd shouldered a Geelong player. One spectator accidentally ran into me and came off second best. He didn't mean to engage in a front-on collision, but he ended up on the deck.

Such was the impact, his wallet fell out of his pocket. I retrieved it for him so he could buy beers in the Paddington Inn later, and I left the field. The match was temporarily halted while the crowd cleared and Buddy was returned safely to the Swans' rooms. How he eventually made it there, I'll never know.

When the match resumed, lifted by the enormity of the occasion, the Swans won by 30 points. Despite the defeat, we outperformed them in a number of key areas, so we weren't perturbed. This was one of those rare occasions where I was able to see more positives than negatives, even though we had lost.

Considering the way the season turned out, and who we

defeated in the final, I'm happy Buddy had his moment, even if the game turned into a shemozzle and then a defeat for us.

We also lost to Hawthorn in round five, but I didn't think there was any cause for concern. Overall, we were trending well. I was feeling good about where we were at ... until round seven.

In round seven, we lost to Fremantle by three points, at home.

Now, bear in mind that, after our horror showing against the Demons in the prelim only a few months earlier, I was, for about twelve hours, ready to retire. Let's just say those feelings about my footy mortality and how our group was going, started to resurface. I thought Fremantle was a poor side, which was unfair to them. They actually finished the season fifth on the ladder but, at the time, I was horrified.

How the fuck did we lose to Fremantle right now? And at home? What is going on with us? As always, consumed by the obsession with winning a Premiership. *That's it, if we can't beat them at home, we're never winning this thing. If you lose to Freo at GMHBA, you're not beating Collingwood or Melbourne, when it counts, at the G.*

Season over, in my mind.

I was starting to become sour, almost resentful – resentful of footy in general. The game was starting to weigh me down in a way it never had before.

Over the next few days, I couldn't get out of my funk. I messaged James Kelly and asked if he would be free for a coffee. We met at a café called Blank Space to talk about the blank space in my trophy cabinet, in a career that I felt was close to the end.

'Don't be like me,' James said, after I explained my concerns for the group, my disappointment about how we were playing and how far off a Premiership I thought we were, as well as my fears that 2022 would be my last season.

Don't be like him? He was a three-time Premiership player and an All-Australian to boot. If only!

'In my last season at Geelong, before moving to Essendon, I was that grumpy older player that no one wants to be around. I'm pretty sure some of the younger players would have thought I was an asshole.'

Wow, I thought. *Is that what I was turning into?*

I thought I was rightly concerned about our form, and so I should be. Then, I thought about how I'd punched the wall after our prelim defeat to Melbourne and screamed to a level that had shocked my teammates. That wasn't my usual way. Was I changing?

'If you do what I did, the main thing you'll miss out on is enjoyment. I cost myself that in my last season playing here. I'll never get that year back. You can't control how much time you have left in your career, but you can control how you show up. If you're positive, you'll enjoy it more.'

He had a point. It wasn't enjoyable being a grumpy fucker.

'If you don't like how we're playing – and remember there are a lot of new coaches this year so it takes time for a new plan to click, but it will – why don't you play like you're an ambassador for how you want the team to play?'

As always, James was right.

I've since asked him why he didn't just tell me to cop on and stop being a downer on the group. He said he didn't want to shame me into being cheerful, he actually wanted me to enjoy my football. He said if I was enjoying my football, it would be good for the team.

This is an example of what makes Kell such a great coach. He retired at the age of 33, so had empathy for the plight of the older player. And he has a way of delivering a message that ensures it hits just right. If he worked in media, he'd be a Gerard Whateley.

That conversation changed my whole approach. I went to work on Monday with a new attitude. I'll always be grateful to him for that. I mean, no one wants a grumpy Reggie in the change room. I was sick of grumpy Reggie. It was time to bring the fun back.

A week later, we hammered GWS by 53 points. We had one more setback after that. A loss to St Kilda by 10 points. We didn't know it at the time, but that loss at Marvel Stadium in round nine was our last for the year. We went on to win the next 16 in a row, including playing St Kilda again in round 21 when we hammered them by 45 points.

In round 19, we defeated Port Adelaide in Adelaide. That, for me, was the game that solidified it all, I knew we could win the flag after that.

It was a game of wild swings of momentum. We led by 34 points at half-time. It should have been a done deal, but Port kicked eight goals to one in the third quarter and led by seven points going into the final term. There's no way we should have gone on to win from there, but we did. As he so often did, Hawk (Tom Hawkins) rose to the occasion, kicking two of his four-goal haul in the final quarter. We ended up winning by 12 points.

That game is memorable because of the contrast with how I felt after the early-season loss to Fremantle. I walked off the ground with Patrick Dangerfield and told him what the win meant.

'We're going to win it. We are definitely the best in the competition,' I said.

I just felt like it was a game that we shouldn't have won, but we did. Playing at Adelaide Oval is tough. Port Adelaide fans are feral, and I mean that as a compliment as the atmosphere they create is electrifying. It's a special experience. We had won there against the odds. This had to be our year; I was sure of it.

It felt like we were making opposition teams buckle under pressure. For a time, they could stay with us but, if they didn't take their limited opportunities, we'd break their spirits by cruising home and winning the game. That's how the end of that year felt.

We headed into a finals campaign in red-hot form, with 13 consecutive wins. We would go on to beat Collingwood in our qualifying final in what would be one of the toughest games of my career.

Collingwood were in front with just five minutes to go after Jordan De Goey kicked his second goal of the match. Then up stepped Gary Rohan, literally. I had taken an intercept mark and kicked it in his direction. He took a massive pack mark and converted it into a long-range set-shot (free kick) goal. It was never in doubt. He is technically one of the best set shots I've ever seen, so we were in safe hands. But it was, nevertheless, impressive to watch in real time.

With just a few minutes remaining, the footy was bouncing around our half-back line in front of the Shane Warne Stand when I lunged at it to try to nudge it towards a teammate. I was desperately trying to get it to Tom Stewart. He ended up winning the ball, then kicking to Cam Guthrie, who passed it to Jeremy Cameron on the wing, who in turn delivered it to Gary Rohan – at least he tried to. Gary didn't mark it, but in the spill that followed, Max Holmes was the beneficiary as he ran into an open goal to kick the match sealer. It was a huge moment, and it turned out to be the victory that won us a Premiership. Unfortunately for Max, he ended up missing out on the final because of injury. A devastating turn of events for a player that had helped us win the toughest match of the finals series.

I do admit, although it pains me, as I don't like giving Collingwood credit, that the qualifying final was probably the toughest win of my life. After the victory, I ran to the crowd punching my chest. Straight away, I knew the significance of it.

We smashed Brisbane in the preliminary final to the tune of 71 points. They had beaten Richmond and Melbourne on their way to the prelim and, after a couple of big performances, it seemed like they just couldn't back it up mentally. They didn't turn up at the G, which was fucking great for us. I couldn't have been happier to inflict that beating on them.

At this point in my career, my dislike of Brisbane, as previously discussed, was at an all-time high. During your career, the level to which you dislike certain teams ebbs and flows, or at least it does for me. I didn't have many thoughts on Brisbane for a long time – they were pretty inoffensive – but by 2022 they were officially on top of my list of disdain. Beating them had become my favourite thing to do, especially after Harris Andrews' outburst in 2021. Hopefully, he was impressed with our performance on this occasion.

The sweet taste of that cold revenge was a big season highlight, but it was actually rounds 20 and 21, and the serendipitous nature of events surrounding them, that shaped my experience of the Grand Final.

Stick with me while I backtrack a little and explain.

In round 20, we were playing the Western Bulldogs at home and we were celebrating Joel Selwood's 350th game.

It was a massive occasion for the club. On the Tuesday leading into the match, I wasn't feeling great. I had a bit of a sniffle. I did a Covid test and left it on the bench before getting into the shower. When I returned to the kitchen, Bec was staring at the test and then at me.

She looked devastated. 'You have Covid.'

I was so impressed at how distraught she looked. She knew how much I hated missing games, that this match was a big deal for the club and that I'd be filthy to miss out. What a fiancée! As it turned out, that's not why she was upset.

What I didn't know was that Bec had planned a very special surprise and this Covid test had thrown a major spanner in the works.

The following day, Bec took Rafferty to work with her. She said she didn't want him getting Covid. She wasn't due to work that day, but she told me she had a photo shoot. This wasn't unusual in her role as a fashion sales and brand manager, so I didn't question it.

When 7 p.m. came and passed without hearing anything from her, I started to panic. She wasn't answering her phone, which was really unusual, and it was getting late for Rafferty to be out. I contacted one of her colleagues to check if everything was okay, but they had no idea. They said Bec had left work at the usual time. What was going on? I thought she was at a photo shoot. At this point, I was freaking out. I'm not a worrier, compared to Bec, but here I was imagining all sorts of worst-case scenarios.

A short time later, she finally arrived, after ignoring about 10 of my phone calls. 'Don't be mad,' she said. 'I have a special delivery.'

What sort of delivery?

Following her into the kitchen were Mammy and Daddy.

There were awkward masked hugs as I realised why Bec had been so upset by my positive Covid test. She had been busy arranging accommodation for them as they couldn't stay with us until I had recovered.

That wasn't the end of the surprise deliveries. Just a few minutes later, as I was getting my head around Mammy and Daddy's arrival, I saw more people at the patio door. Surely not? In walked Naomi, her husband Noel, and their kids, Ava, Lucy, Laila and Mia Rose. The whole crew was here. Unbelievable.

Bec explained that she couldn't answer the phone in the car as she was certain Rafferty would blurt out the fact Nanna and Grandpa were there and ruin the surprise. He was so excited to see them – and that's exactly what he would have done.

Ironically, they all attended Joel's milestone match, and I didn't. They had a great time. I was gutted, but there was a silver lining on the way.

A week later, we were playing St Kilda. I had got over Covid and, the night before, I was eating my usual pre-match pasta. Bec had cooked up a delicious chicken risoni bake, and I was devouring it.

All of a sudden, I started to feel unusually full. This was odd – I can eat endless supplies of pasta. Then, my stomach started to cramp. Surely not. Had I caught the stomach bug Flynn and Rafferty had during the week? I must have. I certainly hadn't been near a jacuzzi.

I went to bed and hoped for the best. Spoiler alert, the best did not happen. I ejected the pasta bake in a gruesome episode shortly after. In addition to not being able to keep any food down, I also started to burn up. It was a quickly evolving gastro situation.

As you'll know by now, I pride myself on not missing matches for any reason, so I got up the next day and packed my kit bag as always. When I got to the ground, the medical staff asked if I felt like I was fit to play. I immediately said that, yes, I was. They told me I'd have to do a fitness test.

The test involves some shuttle sprints and wrestling. I made it through those, just about, but I was burning up. I felt awful. But I couldn't bring myself to miss the game. My ethos, as always, was play unless you physically can't, and, technically, I could, so I did. It's crazy when I look back on it. They let me have the final call on it, but I'm sure they could see how pale I was.

My first few efforts were sub-par. I felt horrible – lethargic and slow. I managed to kick a goal early on – I got through and we won – but it wasn't fun.

It was extra special to have my dad there. A trip down here is a big effort with his health, and for him to do that meant a lot. Had they come out just a couple of weeks later and seen our qualifying final win, I'm sure they would have extended their trip in the hope that we went on to win the flag. Or if Dad was fully healthy, they might have flown back out to Australia again. But it wasn't to be. I'll always be grateful that they got to see me play for 'Peak Geelong', which is what we were at that stage. We were humming.

A week later, we thrashed the Gold Coast Suns by 60 points.

The day after, on 14 August at the Old Treasury Building in East Melbourne, Bec and I got 'officially' married with our families watching on. It was a busy few weeks. Bec had arranged to bring the ceremony forward so my family could be there. Another lovely surprise in what was turning into my favourite year. (Don't worry, there was still a big wedding party scheduled for Ireland.)

Now for the reason I'm backtracking. Why is the missed match due to Covid and pushing through gastro relevant? What I didn't realise at the time was that I was heading for the most significant milestone yet.

Thanks to the precise number of games I had played up to that moment, the Grand Final would end up being my 250th game. Now, we just had to win it.

CHAPTER 9

Head in the Game

I HAD TWO THEORIES ABOUT HOW THE GRAND Final could go.

Sydney had the potential to win it, for sure. But, if they did, it would be a tough, close contest and the margin would be small. That was a best-case scenario for them. If they didn't bring their absolute best on the day, we could thrash them. I was convinced of that.

By the time Grand Final week rolled around, I had convinced myself that even the latter scenario was a huge negative. How could thinking we had the potential to thrash the opposition in the Grand Final be a negative? Well, if you overthink any situation for long enough, you can turn it into one.

The more I thought about it, the more nervous I became, and the more I knew I had to take action.

For the first time ever, I contacted the club psychologist and asked for a session. Bear in mind, there had been times in my career before then that I'd been given a psychologist's number and never used it. I'd cried in my car on the side of the road every day after training, for months on end, and even that wasn't enough to drive me to a psych. But the prospect of losing a Grand Final did.

For what it's worth, if one of my sons came to me saying they were struggling, I'd be devastated if they didn't want to talk to someone about it. I've been educated on that and I know it's the right thing to do.

I booked an appointment with 'Big Cat', aka David Williams, the club psychologist. He's a legend and a gentle giant.

'The Richmond Grand Final was different to this one,' I said. 'I knew, for us to beat them, we would have to be at our best. But we are so much better than Sydney and, if we let this one slip, I won't cope. I can't even bear the thought of it. If I couldn't deal with losing to Melbourne in a prelim and I almost retired, how would I deal with that?'

I look back on it now and laugh. To be nervous because you think you're so much better than a team might sound odd, but it was a genuine concern.

'The fact you're anxious about how good you think your team is is a good thing,' Dave reassured me.

Big Cat has a way of talking you down and rationalising things. He's all about managing your self-talk and your perception. He managed to stop me catastrophising a worst-case scenario and assured me that it's only as big as you make it in your mind. My mind had made that worst-case scenario quite the episode.

It was around this time that I referenced notes I'd taken on a team Zoom we did with former All Blacks captain and rugby legend Richie McCaw back in 2020. He'd spoken to the team about dealing with anxiety in the build-up to big matches. In New Zealand, where rugby is a religion, the pressure to win World Cups was huge, so if anyone knew about dealing with heightened expectation, it was him.

He told us he used a simple strategy. Before playing in the World Cup final, he would ask himself, 'If I could only ever play one more game of rugby, which one would I choose?' There was only ever one answer.

Of course, he would want to play in the Rugby World Cup final. If that's all you've ever wanted, why would you be anxious? He ended up winning two.

I was doing my best not to let my anxiety ruin the Grand Final, but it wasn't easy.

The truth was, it's all I had ever wanted, and I had become obsessive about it since joining the Cats.

I didn't just think about it all the time, I'd said it publicly in interviews. In one chat with Irish journalist Maurice Brosnan on *The 42* podcast at the end of the 2021 season, I admitted something I had never said out loud. Maurice asked me how I would measure success at the end of my career.

It is hard not to think fairly deeply about these things when you are my age. I am fully aware I am going to have fewer and fewer opportunities from here on in. It is hard to dedicate yourself physically and emotionally to trying to win a flag. If, at the end of it all, you don't win it, I'm just not sure how I could ever view myself as a success. Failure would be too harsh a word, but success might be going too far the other way.

I'd said it. My career would not be a success if I didn't win a flag. I said failure would be 'too harsh a word' in that interview, but my anxiety in the build-up to the final suggested that's exactly how I would view it if we didn't win.

The Big Cat conversation wasn't the only significant discussion I was involved in as we approached the big day.

Early in the week, Isaac 'Issie' Smith, Mitch Duncan and I were called into Scotty's office. James Kelly and assistant coach Nigel Lappin were there too. They had a Grand Final plan for the three of us, and they wanted to brief us on it.

Scotty was going to start me down back, with Issie moving to the wing and Mitch playing at half-forward. Then, after around 10 minutes, we would all rotate. I would move to the wing, Issie would slide forward and Mitch would end up down back.

This plan was concocted because we were certain the Swans were going to tag Tom Stewart, which would make it hard for us to free him up to play as the spare. Because they would invest so much time in Tom (and why wouldn't they – he'd won four All-Australians at this point, including in 2022), we needed to have a plan to counteract them.

I've always loved being part of plans like these because it signified to me that the coaches trusted me to deliver. I wanted to be part of this one when it counted most – on Grand Final Day. However, I was slightly apprehensive. I had only played this role once during the year, in the second half against a poor West Coast Eagles side – the Grand Final would be a very different proposition.

There was plenty of excitement back in Ireland in the build-up to the final. My sister Naomi and her brother-in-law David decided to fly out to Australia for the big day. When I say they flew out together, this isn't strictly true. Somehow, in the excitement of booking flights to watch her little brother play in a Grand Final, Naomi had booked

David on a later flight for the second leg, so when they got to Abu Dhabi, she continued to Melbourne without him. He had seven extra hours to fill at the airport so, when Naomi arrived in Melbourne, she had a short rest before going back to the airport to collect him. They pretty much went straight from the baggage carousel to the Grand Final parade. We still laugh about it now. She insists she didn't do it on purpose – personally, I wouldn't blame her if she did.

If they had missed the 2022 Grand Final parade, it wouldn't have been the worst thing ever. This was the year the AFL decided to take the parade off the streets and onto the river – with mixed reviews, it must be said. Perhaps they were still slightly motivated by social distancing and ensuring the players made it to the final in good health. It certainly made for a more relaxing experience. We just stood on the boat talking shit to each other.

The parade is an event I've watched so often on TV. It was surreal to go from being on the couch as a spectator to being in it. Because of Covid restrictions and the location, there hadn't been a Grand Final parade in the build-up to the 2020 decider, so it was cool to finally experience it, even if it was on the river. It reminded me of the feeling I got when I first saw 'Grand Final 2020' written on my jumper the last time around. It's hard to process that it's you getting that opportunity.

One thing I did notice was the number of Irish flags on

the banks of the Yarra. Mark O'Connor and I were blown away by that. It was special to have an Irish teammate to experience it with, and I'll forever be grateful to Irish AFL fans who turned up to support us – not just that day, but on the many occasions I looked up into the stands only to see the tricolour proudly displayed.

Irish flags had been popping up in the crowd more and more in Geelong. It made sense – the Irish were taking over. At the Cattery, Irish people were like mice. If you saw one of us in the kitchen, you could be sure there were another couple of us near the couch.

Because of the club's infamous social-media post announcing my impending arrival when I was first traded, which featured an Ivory Coast flag, I still half expected to see one of those in the crowd too, but, thankfully, that hadn't caught on.

I stayed in the Pullman Hotel the night before the final. The club gave us the option, and I took it. The traffic would be chaotic the morning of the match and, perhaps in one final throwback to my Carlton days, I still had a slight phobia of lateness.

I slept well that night and was able to get through a big breakfast, which was a great sign. I don't usually eat in the morning, apart from on main training days and game day, when I want to fuel properly. I initially started skipping breakfast as a method of keeping my weight down but, over time, it became a habit. If I can eat breakfast easily, without having to force it down, I know I'm in good form. When I'm nervous, it's a struggle.

On Grand Final morning, I had a healthy portion of eggs on toast with bacon and avocado on the side. I remember thinking how delicious it was and how effective my talk with Big Cat had been. The only emotion I was feeling was excitement. Pure excitement.

I decided to go for a stroll around Albert Park Lake – Irish readers, you'll know it from watching the Australian Grand Prix. The club advises we go for a walk on match day to start the process of loosening up. It was an idyllic Melbourne day. The sky was bright blue, the sun was out, the lake was glistening. As I meandered around, an athlete sprinted past.

I thought, *I know that guy. Was that ...? Yes, it was.*

It was Sam Docherty. My good friend and former teammate at the Blues, who had been there for me in so many of the ups and the downs. The man that came up with the nickname 'Reggie'. He ran past me so fast when I first saw him that I knew he was in the middle of sprint repetitions he needed to finish, so it had to be a short chat.

'How are you?' he said.

I was good. But this meeting had reminded me of everything that could have been. When I joined the Blues, I thought I'd never leave. I wanted to be a one-club player so badly. Imagine if I hadn't left. Sam Docherty was there when I agonised over the decision, when I'd shed tears outside a Portlaoise bar, wondering if I was doing the right thing. Carlton hadn't made the finals and Sam was back in pre-season training already. Meanwhile, I was preparing for my second Grand Final.

It was a huge reality check. *How lucky am I?*

Sam wished me the best for the match and kept running.

I returned to the hotel and had my usual pre-match chicken sandwich for lunch in the team room. Again, there was no need to force it down. I was eating well. I knew I was ready.

Grand Final Day is the biggest day of the year in Melbourne. You're either going to the Grand Final or you're watching at the pub or you're going to a friend's barbeque – or you hate the two teams playing so much that you don't watch at all. But everyone is involved and invested in some way.

This Grand Final Day was more significant than usual. There hadn't been a Grand Final at the MCG for two years. Because of Covid, the 2020 decider that we lost to Richmond had been at the Gabba in Brisbane, and in 2021 it had been staged in Perth. Melbournians had been starved of the biggest day on the footy calendar, and now it was back.

They say absence makes the heart grow fonder, and that was certainly the case with the G on Grand Final Day. It looked radiant. As we approached on the bus, it was gleaming. It was a pristine day – just perfect for football.

I had an American heavy-metal band called Pantera streaming through my AirPods during the bus journey. 'Cowboys from Hell' and 'Cemetery Gates' were my chosen songs, and I wanted to bury the Swans' title hopes.

They're not just wicked pump-up songs. I like a blast from the past in my ears when I'm preparing for big games. It helps evoke that feeling of when I was growing up and sport was just for fun. It also reminds me of how far I've come.

It was my brother Noel John who first introduced me to Pantera. I thought of how proud he would be to know that on the biggest day of my career, he was still the strongest influence on my playlist. When I first started listening to 'Cowboys from Hell' there were no AirPods. Back then, I had a Discman and would listen through my headphones as I walked to Downey's, our local shop. A lot had changed, but a lot had stayed the same.

I don't always indulge in heavy metal. Sometimes, Irish singer Damien Rice is top of my playlist. The live version of 'Colour Me In' is a go-to track when driving to matches.

And, yes, if you pop that song on your Spotify playlist, you might be surprised. It's very romantic, perhaps not how you imagine I would prepare, but as I'm sure you've picked up in this book, I have a romantic side – just ask Bec!

Grand Final Day, however, was not a Damien Rice day. It was a heavy, heavy metal kind of day.

The pre-match entertainment wasn't in the heavy-metal genre, but it was legendary. Robbie Williams was booked to perform and crowds had made sure they were seated extra early to take in the show. There had been speculation that Kylie Minogue might make an appearance but, in the end, it was Delta Goodrem who joined him on stage.

I'm a big Robbie Williams fan. It was weird to be in a situation where someone of his stature was playing a gig just metres away that you could watch for free, but that you can't really watch as you're preparing for the biggest match of your life.

When he took to the field, we were downstairs in the warm-up area, doing our best to at least keep an eye on the TV screens, but the soundproofing meant that, even though he was just above us, we couldn't hear a thing. He was wearing a bright-pink suit that popped on screen. I watched him on TV while waiting in line to be strapped for the game. He and Delta got a warm reception from the crowd. If we could perform as well as them, our fans would be happy at the end of the day.

My first glimpse of the hallowed turf that day was just before watching our teammate, Shannon Neale, compete in the traditional Grand Final sprint. A player from each team in the league gets to race as part of the preamble. Our man Shannon won his heat and made the final, though he didn't win the decider and finished sixth. Not bad for a 6' 6" dude. He had outdone himself. We had a great laugh watching him and we were proud. It was a nice distraction from what was to come.

The air was crisp and infused with anticipation and, coupled with Robbie's performance, the vibe was pumping. I've no idea how it compared to other Grand Finals, as I had never been to one as a spectator. The only Grand Final I'd attended was the 2020 iteration at the Gabba. I'd had the opportunity to go before – I'd been invited, and even had some previous coaches urge me to go and get a feel for what it might be like, but quite frankly, fuck that. Why would I go and watch another team win a Premiership?

Sounds masochistic to me.

Mick Malthouse and Brendon Bolton had both advised us to attend a final while I was at Carlton, but I never did. Then the closer you get to playing in one, the harder it is to go. For example, if you lose a prelim, why would you go and watch the final? It would make me sick to see the team I'd lost to play on the big stage and, even worse, win it.

I never had the urge to go, and I'm glad I didn't. I was very content to experience my first Grand Final at the MCG as a player with that 'Grand Final 2022' crest on my jumper. That's the only way I wanted to 'Grand Final' as a player. In retirement, I'm sure that will change. I'd love to take Flynn and Rafferty to a decider the Cats are playing in one day.

I've always backed myself to deal with the big stage. I had

dealt with my nerves earlier in the week but, even if I hadn't, no matter how nervous I have been before matches, the second the ball is bounced, those feelings have dissipated.

As you know, I'm also not a believer in having to feel good to play well. I've played when I've been injured or down and out, and still performed. Whenever I've felt nerves, I've reminded myself of the fact that, even if I didn't feel great, I had the ability to deliver.

I'm pleased to say that on Grand Final Day, in the biggest match I had ever played, I was in the zone. On that beautiful last Saturday in September, it wasn't just me, it felt like the whole team was.

The first 10 minutes of the match were weird. Despite an abundance of possession, it took us nine minutes to score. You'd think we'd be worried but, conversely, even though we hadn't kicked a goal yet, I knew the game was ours for the taking. We were completely in control and peppering them, it was just a matter of time.

Scotty's plan for Isaac, Mitch and me was working well too. While we only planned to play that way for the first 10 minutes, when I went to the interchange bench, I was instructed the play would stay that way. We wouldn't rotate, I was staying as a deep spare. It was only supposed to be until we sussed out where Sydney was at, but it was already proving to be effective. Hearing this message on the bench was another indicator that things were going our way. I ended up playing deep spare all day.

Despite the relative lack of scores, there were some big moments in the first quarter. In the first minute of the match, I won an early contest. I beat Isaac Heeney to the ball on the wing and kicked inside 50 to Hawk, who marked it.

My compatriot Mark 'Mez' O'Connor also made his presence felt in that first term. He had come into the side to replace the unlucky Max Holmes, who had injured his hamstring in the preliminary final against Brisbane and run out of time to recover. Mez was making the most of his opportunity – that was evident straightaway.

We were 19 points up, and the Swans were on the counterattack. James Rowbottom was in space and hurtling towards the forward 50. Just as he dropped the ball to his foot, Mez came from nowhere and ran him down. The 'holding the ball' decision went our way, and the resulting turnover culminated in Isaac Smith's second consecutive goal.

You look at that and you just know: it's our game. You might think it's easy to say that in hindsight and, because the game was a complete blowout, those moments were bigger than they appeared – but it was huge. We now led by 25 points.

Having not scored for the first nine minutes, we kicked six consecutive goals to lead by 35 points at quarter-time. The Swans tried to claw their way back but we maintained a 36-point lead at half-time.

It's time to make an admission about the Sydney Swans

– along with the Brisbane Lions, they are the team I dislike the most.

The Swans are a bit of a paradox for me, don't get me wrong. I have a huge amount of respect for how long they have been able to remain competitive. I think Geelong and Sydney are the two clear standouts in that space in the modern era. But there is a strut, a bravado, associated with the Swans that has always rubbed me up the wrong way.

I thought that, after half-time, they might try to start something. I expected them to come out with their chests puffed out and with an extra bit of grunt, to maybe even start a blue to get themselves back in the contest or to try to distract us. I expected them to come out and start roughing us up.

As we walked back out of the rooms for the second half, I warned my teammates of the dangers of this. 'If they start anything, just walk away,' I said. This was rich coming from me, I know, as I've been known to 'embrace' opposition angst. But this second half of football was too important to get involved in bullshit like that.

Much to my surprise, the Swans didn't do any of that. The second half carried on from where the first half finished. The first passage of play, in my mind, effectively ended the contest.

Sydney spilled possession and Gary Rohan mopped it up, spinning out of a tackle to deliver it to Mark 'Blitz' Blicavs. Blitz snapped it forward, but neither Isaac Smith nor Jez

(Jeremy Cameron) could get clean hands on it – instead Tom McCartin gained possession. But, in another moment that epitomised our effort that day, Mitch Duncan ran him down and was paid (awarded) a 'holding the ball' free kick.

For Irish readers, the 'holding the ball' rule is one of the most contentious in the AFL. A free kick is awarded to the opposition of any player who fails to correctly dispose of the football after being tackled by an opponent. This rule, and the recent tweaks to it, has resulted in AFL crowds incessantly chanting 'balllllllllll' if they perceive an opposition player has not disposed of the ball correctly. If you visit Australia and watch a game of footy, you'll hear 'balllllll' from the crowd almost as much as you'll hear them cheer.

Anyway, Duncan duly converted that free kick. *Dream stuff*, I thought. If they had come out and executed that exact passage of play, it could have resurrected their chances. But they didn't.

I look back now and sympathise with them. When games are so far gone, when the opposition is so dominant in every area, it's difficult to turn it around. While that first goal of the half was a huge dent in their attempt to wrestle back any kind of momentum, the next goal was, in my view, the sealer. And it was early in the third quarter.

Brad Close took an intercept mark from a Tom McCartin kickout gone wrong and kicked the goal. At that exact point, it felt like the Swans' spirits were broken. They were completely demoralised and didn't kick a goal for the entire quarter. We kicked six – they only managed a solitary behind.

Even I, as a perennial pessimist, who is always barking 'we need to stay on here', knew it was over. It was now a training run, with a party on the side.

The further we went into the lead, the more we allowed ourselves to celebrate. It was raining goals and, after each one, we celebrated as a team. I would point to where I knew my family was in the stand. I thought about what my sister would be thinking of it all. From sending me money via Western Union, to this. I thought about my parents back home. My mother was so notoriously bad at watching matches, but we were so far ahead that maybe even she would be watching the second half?

It turned out she only watched the last 10 or 15 minutes. That is how bad a spectator she is! Which is probably where I get it from. I don't suffer from nerves at all when I'm on the field but if I have to watch the Cats from the stand, my anxiety is through the roof.

Being able to enjoy the moment while still in the match was not something I had imagined. I knew we had the ability to smash them, but I hadn't envisaged being so far ahead that we could take it all in and enjoy the process of it.

At three-quarter-time, our skipper told it as it was. As he always did.

'We have it won. Let's just enjoy this last quarter, boys,'

Joel smiled as he delivered my favourite three-quarter-time peptalk of all time. 'But don't forget – you'll always remember this last 30 minutes, how we finish this game will stick with you forever.'

Scotty was there and went along with it. 'Yes, okay, go for it.'

Can you actually believe it? We got to 'just enjoy' the last quarter of the Grand Final. That is literally what footy dreams are made of.

The skipper certainly enjoyed himself. In what would turn out to be his last game for the club, and his first Premiership as a Cats captain, Joel kicked what would have to be just about the best goal of his career. Celebrating his goal as a team is one of my favourite moments from that match.

Jeremy Cameron was also enjoying himself. He kicked our final goal to contribute to what would end up being an 81-point win.

No one enjoys kicking a goal more than Jez. People often ask me what he's like. What he's like is just one of those people who is brilliant at football. That's it. There's no science behind it, he's just a freakishly good footballer. Jez has the unique ability to never allow a temporary problem to change his attitude. On the rare occasion where he may be a bit wayward with his goal-kicking, he can smile it off knowing full well that he'll kick the next. And if he doesn't, well then, he'll just kick the one after that, and so on.

He's just Jezza. What you see is what you get. He plays a bit of golf, looks after the cows on his farm, and then goes and kicks a bag on the MCG on the weekend. Simple.

As for the game plan that Scotty, James and Nigel had orchestrated in our meeting during the week? We had stuck with that structure all day, and it worked a treat. I anchored our defence, Mitch was instrumental further up the ground and Issie, well, he took home the Norm Smith medal – best player on the ground in the Grand Final – which says it all.

All three players who sat in Scotty's office had made a significant impact on the outcome of the game. Another sign, if it was needed, of just how good our coaches were.

I'll never forget the feeling of knowing I was about to do what I'd always wanted to do – win a Grand Final. To beat Brisbane in the prelim and Sydney in the final, by a lot – to beat the two teams I like the least, by a lot … fucking hell. Inject that feeling into me.

There were about 20 seconds to go in the match, and it had been clear for a while that it was absolutely over, beyond doubt. I looked over at the interchange bench and saw that the coaches had come down from the box and were hugging each other. They were starting to celebrate. It was real. A wave of emotion swept over me.

It's difficult to put into words what it feels like to achieve a dream like that.

I almost wrote 'lifelong dream', but that isn't true.

There were two players on the field that day who had grown up with very different dreams.

I grew up wanting to play for Liverpool or Laois. I dreamed of scoring the winning goal in the FA Cup final or in the All-Ireland decider. When my soccer dreams didn't materialise, Croke Park, on the biggest day of all, became my focus. But then along came AFL and, for years, I'd had a different dream. And it had finally happened.

Mark O'Connor was in the same situation. Having grown up wanting to lift the Sam Maguire Cup with Kerry (that's the trophy you win if you're victorious in the All-Ireland final), he too had achieved a dream he couldn't have fathomed as a child.

To do that together was incredibly special.

I had travelled thousands of miles and lived on the opposite side of the world to my family for this moment. This would justify all of it. Everything I'd missed. Everything I'd given up, to be here. And my sister was in the crowd to see it. Elation doesn't even cover it.

I get goosebumps all over me just thinking about that image of the coaches celebrating. Of them poised on the sideline waiting to run onto the field. The siren was about to sound.

FUCK. IT'S ACTUALLY ABOUT TO HAPPEN.

When it did, tears streamed down my face. Remember how Jack Riewoldt took time to console me after we lost the Grand Final to Richmond in 2020? Well, I could have done with him being at the fence to give me a hug. Having finally done it, after all these years, I needed consoling for a much happier reason.

Every time I think about that Grand Final siren, I'm overcome with emotion. The very thought of it has a tangible physical effect on me.

Photos of myself and Mark O'Connor in the aftermath make me smile every time. For two out of the 22 players in the squad that day to be born thousands of miles away, to have never played Aussie Rules until their late teens, and then to win, was insane.

When I saw Scotty out on the ground, I was emotional. He had been so good to me. I couldn't respect him more, and so to do it for him felt like I was paying him back for the faith he'd shown in me. From trying to impress him at that first meeting at Brad's apartment block to this – who'd have thought?

James Kelly also came over to celebrate and we had to laugh. Remember that coffee I had with him after the loss to Fremantle? The one where I told him we were done for the year? We had no chance.

'I might have gone a little bit early on the whole "season being over" thing,' I chuckled.

'Yes, maybe,' he said with a smile.

And then there was Nigel Lappin, probably the coach whose had the biggest impact on me as far as coaches go. The most genuinely caring coach I've ever had, who was uniquely aware of how bad I had wanted this. He had done everything he could over the course of my Geelong career to help me become the best possible version of myself. Not only as a coach, but also one of my great mates.

What a journey it had been to my first flag. I was never in doubt about how I got there, what had made me the player I was – that was Portlaoise GAA club.

As we waited for the medal presentation, it occurred to me there was an item in my locker I needed urgently. I'd had it in my possession for two years, and I was finally going to have the opportunity to use it.

The Portlaoise flag I held up on stage wasn't new. I'd had it made for the 2020 Grand Final. I'd found a green and white flag and approached my teammate at the time, Quinton Narkle, who is a talented artist, to ask him if he would paint the letters for 'C'mon the Town' on it. That's the catch-cry of our Portlaoise GAA supporters at home. The flag itself was actually a Nigerian flag, it's the same colour scheme and worked well in lieu of waiting to have one sent over from Ireland. Quinton did a great job. I'd kept it in my kit bag for the 2020 Grand Final in the hope we could cause an upset and beat Richmond. When that didn't happen, it stayed in my wardrobe at home for two years, only coming out to go into my bag for my second Grand Final.

I was so overwhelmed by the fact that we'd won, I'd almost forgotten to retrieve it. I was chatting to the medical team when I remembered.

'Can one of you please go to locker number two and take out the green and white flag that's folded up in the back?' I asked.

Embarrassingly, I can't remember exactly who got it for me, it's all a blur, but it was in my hand in a matter of minutes. I spent time ensuring it was the right way around so when I unrolled in on stage it wouldn't say 'nwoT ɘdʇ nom'Ɔ' while I proudly displayed it. It was my time to thank my club, to give them the credit they deserved.

'C'mon the Town' on the Grand Final stage at the MCG – I have no words for what that means to me. As I unrolled the flag, I was looking up to where my sister and brother-in-law were sitting. I get chills when I think of that.

Getting your Premiership medallion is a huge moment. The first thing that struck me when the Auskick (a national program run by the AFL to promote and facilitate children playing AFL) member handed it over was just how heavy it was. How ironic that the moment the weight of pressure of a long-term goal evaporates from your shoulders, it is replaced with a much more pleasant weight around your neck. I couldn't stop looking at it and playing with it. I've never been so obsessed with a piece of 'jewellery'.

The presentation also provided moments of comedy. Like poor Tom Stewart's attempt to collect his medal. The running order of events is, you give the kid presenting the medal a baseball cap and they hand you your medal. Then, you shake hands. Simple. Not so much so for Stewie. He somehow managed to sabotage a couple of steps in this process: first of all leaving the kid hanging when she went to shake hands and then knocking the hat off her head with his celebration. It might've been my all-time favourite Tom Stewart highlight. What made it worse was that he's number 44, so he was the last player to go up on stage. How did he not learn from all 21 players who had gone up before him? Hilarious.

My favourite moment of all was turning around to see Bec, Flynn and Rafferty running towards me. It was chaos after the match, and while I knew they were bringing the families down, I didn't know they'd arrived. I'll never forget the look on the kids' faces. Rafferty kissed me on the nose and Flynn was as obsessed with my medal as I was. He had desperately wanted to see a medal up close after the Grand Final in 2020, but I'd had to explain that to play with one of those medals, your dad has to win one. Finally, I had done that for him.

The medal will remain tucked away in a drawer, safe from prying eyes, and certainly won't be displayed somewhere in my house for all to see. That's not really my thing. The medal itself isn't actually that important – it's what it represents. It's the culmination of all the good and all the bad times in my career. It will continue to be hidden away until a guest requests an inspection or I gift it permanently to my parents, which is almost certainly where it will live out its days, at their home in Portlaoise.

After I'd brandished my 'C'mon the Town' flag on stage, a Geelong fan helped me continue to put the club on the map. A man in the crowd called Ed Harcourt had gone to the effort of getting his own Portlaoise flag designed. He had got in touch with Portlaoise GAA to organise a copy of the logo and had it printed to bring to the Grand Final. I could see it waving behind the goals we were playing into in the last quarter. It was surreal. A Portlaoise GAA flag at the MCG. I couldn't believe someone would go to the trouble of doing that.

I met him at the boundary, and he took the flag off the stick he'd used to hoist it high into the air and handed it to me so I could wear it. I draped it over my shoulders as we walked around the ground celebrating. Thanks to him, the photo was printed on newspapers and online all over Ireland.

The fact that it was a Portlaoise flag really resonated with people. Our local club is everything to us. The Portlaoise flag going viral on Grand Final Day is everything the GAA is about. Because you're always a club player. Whether you go on to be a county star or you move to another sport, the club is where it all started.

I will always be grateful to Ed for making that flag and for allowing me to celebrate with it. In 2020, we learned, in the strongest terms, that sport is nothing without fans. I'll always be indebted to Ed for providing that full-circle moment.

While I was on the ground at the MCG, I did try to call my parents and they, of course, answered. The connection was poor and, although it was hard to hear what they were saying, the message was coming through loud and clear from both sides – we did it!

When we left the field, I was chaired off to celebrate the milestone of my 250th game. If there's a better way to celebrate, I can't imagine what that is. I had been so miserable on my 200th, because we had lost and because Bec and the kids were in quarantine. This was epic. And all because of that match I missed with Covid. It felt like it was meant to be.

I got chaired off by Rhys Stanley and Mark O'Connor, two of my best mates. Mark's face was unfortunately smothered by the Portlaoise flag during that chair off and, as a result, he doesn't feature as heavily in the photos as maybe he'd like to.

We stayed at the MCG for about two hours celebrating before going back to Geelong. I had a shower (not everyone did!) and, as is traditional, put my sweaty jersey back on over my clothes.

I wore the jersey for days. I don't remember odour being a problem, but there were a lot of drinks involved. As for the medal, I slept with it around my neck. Now I had it, I wasn't letting it out of my sight. When I got in the shower the morning after the Grand Final, my neck was sore from turning the wrong way in bed and sleeping on it.

Often after matches, you don't know exactly where you're sore, it feels like an all-over body experience, until you shower, and you feel that sting from a scratch or a bruise you haven't noticed. I felt that medal injury when the hot water hit my skin. What a great reason to be sore after a match!

It didn't stop me wearing it. After the shower, followed by the application of fresh jeans and a T-shirt, the match-worn jumper and medal went back on for another day of celebrations.

Remember I said that not everyone showered and changed? Not only did Mark Blicavs not get changed out of his match kit, or shower, he literally slept in his football boots and was still wearing them on stage the next day as we were presented to Cats fans. Now that is dedication to an outfit, if ever I've seen it. There were thousands of fans there to see him – and us – with our medals. I highly rate Mark's decision to do that. What a legend. It's exactly the sort of recklessness I'm into. He remained in this outfit when we moved on to Murphys for the after-party.

The day after, we were paraded through Geelong and, again, there were thousands of fans lining the streets as we made our way to a stage on the waterfront. I was overwhelmed by how many people turned out, again. My son Flynn enjoyed it even more than I did.

Mark O'Connor was in the same car as us and as we drove around town, Flynn was excited to hear some of his schoolmates shout out to him as we passed by. Afterwards, he told us that no less than 11 students had spotted him in the parade as he flashed my medal at them! He was in his element.

Our Mad Monday was delayed until the Wednesday, or obvious reasons. If you're reading in Ireland, you might be familiar with the 'Monday Club' and it's basically the same thing. 'Mad Monday' is a massive piss-up after your season finishes, and you wear fancy dress for the occasion.

This year, we all agreed, there was only one way to dress. And that was as old men, leaving their nursing home for a day out. Before the season started, we had been written off by the footy media as just that – too old and past it.

We hadn't done too badly for a team that was considered past it. This is a consistent narrative used against Geelong. Because we don't completely bottom out and engage in rebuilds, instead topping up on talent and ensuring we have senior players to lead younger recruits, the rest of the league wants us to be done. But we rarely are. I quickly found some suitable pieces to wear in a local thrift shop and was ready for the day. It may have been the first time Blicavs took off his footy boots.

In early November, we went back to Ireland. It was time for another important occasion. Bec and I got married on 15 November. Yes, we had done the paperwork in Melbourne, now it was time for the party.

We were less about the formalities and all about the festivities. Our big day was at Ballybeg House in the Wicklow Mountains. It's an old farm property converted into a beautiful venue with accommodation. My sister had got married there eight years earlier, when Flynn was a baby. It was an incredible spot for our celebration. The main country house is made from traditional stone and the interior is all wood and rustic touches. It's next to a small and very picturesque village called Tinahely, where you could go for a drink if you wanted to mix things up over the three-day event.

We wanted it to be intimate, so it was just 50 of our closest friends and family on the day. We rented out the whole place and there was a private shebeen (traditional Irish bar) where we enjoyed a Guinness or two on arrival, and a late-night/early-morning singsong after the ceremony and dinner. If you were so inclined, you could head in there and pull a pint for yourself and sit next to the fire.

It's fair to say that the singsong went on longer than the ceremony. My old man was the celebrant and, honestly, the entirety of the formalities took about seven or eight minutes. We had a couple of speeches over dinner, including my brother's epic Best Man speech, and mine, which I absolutely did not prepare for – opting instead to wing it. It was great.

Ballybeg House is a long way from Geelong, but a few of my teammates made the trip. Rhys Stanley surprised me on the day. He had told me that he couldn't make it – understandably so, his wife Kirsten was pregnant and he was building a house while looking after a young family. He had a lot on his plate. But in the build-up to the big day, Kirsten encouraged him to fly over. She knew that he would regret it if he didn't. He made a last-minute dash. He had told Bec, but they kept it under wraps. The first I knew of it was when I walked into the shebeen and he was there. I couldn't believe it.

He wasn't the only Cat in attendance. Mark Blicavs, Sam Simpson, Jack Henry and Mark O'Connor came too. They had also been to Kerry to watch Mark play Gaelic football for his club, and they'd caused something of a stir, even making it into local media reports. It was quite the Irish tour they were doing.

Portlaoise GAA club organised multiple functions for me too. They did a presentation night with a panel including my former coaches John Mulligan and Mick Lillis, and Mick's son, my good friend Kieran, as well as a former minor (Under-18) teammate of mine, John O'Loughlin. Peter O'Neill, who had been the chairman of the club when I was growing up, made an appearance too, and, of course, one of Laois's all-time great sports people, Pat Critchley.

The effort they went to, and how much my achievements meant to them, blew me away. Before I left Ireland to return to Australia, they unveiled, in the club gym, a huge photo of me with the Portlaoise GAA flag at the MCG on Grand Final Day. It's a permanent fixture.

Not only was it moving to see it, it also helped me come to a major realisation. While I might at one point have been a Carlton player, only to move on and become a Geelong player, I have always, and will always be, a Portlaoise player. In 14 seasons, I had represented the Blues 120 times and the Cats 130 times, but I had represented Portlaoise 250 times.

Turns out, I've been a one-club player my whole life. Just how I always wanted it.

CHAPTER 10

The Irish Experiment

IF I COULD CHANGE ONE THING ABOUT MY AFL career, it would be to have met Jim Stynes. I never did.

Growing up in Ireland, if you've heard of AFL, then you've heard of Jim Stynes. As soon as I heard murmurs there were AFL scouts around, I started looking up Irish players who had followed that path. Locally, Colm Begley had been signed to the Brisbane Lions, and that was huge. I became aware of the name Stynes almost as soon as I became aware of AFL.

But it wasn't until he died in 2012 that I truly understood the impact he'd had.

To put into perspective what Jim Stynes meant to Melbourne and Australia, when he died his family was offered, and accepted, a state funeral.

On the day he was buried, Melbourne stood still as a great of the game was honoured for his life's work, not just on the field but off it too. The legacy of his work with the Reach Foundation meant it wasn't just a celebration of sporting achievement, it was a celebration of those he had impacted away from the sport. The foundation Jim started works with young people to deliver programmes to help build emotional resilience and courage. Today, it works with around 40,000 young people a year.

I had always sensed that Jim was bigger than the game, but on the day of his funeral, 27 March 2012, after a public battle with cancer, it was clear from the magnitude of the occasion that he was so much more than what he achieved in the AFL.

As the 2023 season approached, people started to talk about the possibility that I could surpass Jim's record for the highest number of games played as an Irish player. Jim played 264 matches; I was on 250 at round one.

Despite only being 15 matches away from reaching the milestone, I wasn't taking anything for granted. You have to stay healthy and, in AFL, that's not easy to do. On top of that, the closer the record came, the more surreal it felt. In a way, I didn't want it to happen – I felt like the record should always be his.

But then I started to realise what an honour it would be. With about two weeks to go, I properly weighed it up for the first time.

Jesus I hope I don't get injured now, I thought.

Heading into the week I was due to play my 265th game, I was just relieved to make it there, but I wasn't expecting it to be a big occasion.

It was round 17 of the season, and we were taking on North Melbourne at home. Because it wasn't a traditional milestone – and I'd had a pretty epic 250th celebration – I thought it would pass by without incident. But, in true Geelong fashion, they made sure it didn't.

In the week building up to the match, I was surprised to open up my social media and see that the club had added a moustache to the Geelong logo. They hadn't even told me they were doing it. I couldn't believe my facial hair was featuring on a logo. My moustache had really made it, it's fair to say. I made an extra effort to ensure it was impeccably styled that week to justify such an honour.

Then, the day before the match, the club told me they'd organised for Sam (Jim Stynes' widow) and Tiernan (his son) to be at GMHBA Stadium.

I ran through the banner with Flynn and Rafferty by my side. The kids loved being on the field, especially Flynn, who made a dramatic and surely pre-planned entrance through the banner onto the field, spreading his arms wide

Zach Tuohy

in celebration as he broke through in what is, to this day, among my favourite footage from my career.

We ended up hammering North to the tune of 62 points. The result was meaningful as it meant we were back in the top eight and in finals contention.

Late in the game, I rolled to full-back to take a kick in, and the crowd, sensing the moment, began to cheer, or almost jeer, for a torpedo. It's something I'd become known for and, on special occasions, the crowd craved one even more.

Buckling to peer pressure, I obliged. I can't say it was the purest barrel I've ever hit but it appeased the crowd and seemed like a fitting way to cap things off.

I spoke in the build-up to the game – and in the aftermath for that matter – about the fact that it was strange for me to be placed alongside Jim, even if only statistically. Considering how loved Jim was, I did feel like I was the bad guy in the movie, dethroning a legend. But I must admit, after having the pleasure of meeting and speaking with Sam and Tiernan, my mind was put at ease and I felt much better about the whole situation because of their kindness on the day.

If someone had told me when I first landed at Carlton and was battling away in the VFL, and at one point the VFL reserves, trying to secure senior selection, that I would one day be talking about this record, I would have thought they were crazy.

The club also organised for Sam and Tiernan to present

277

me with one of Jim's Melbourne jumpers after the game. Sam had picked this particular jumper, as it was from a time when 'Tooheys Beer' sponsored the club. I love that about it – what a special touch.

I'm not someone who's collected sports paraphernalia during my career. I'm not especially attached to any of my own jumpers but, to me, Jim's jersey is the most-treasured possession from my 15 AFL seasons. I regularly give away gear, but I will always keep that one.

In a way, every milestone is confronting. The more matches you play, the fewer you have left. I was always pretty good at not dwelling on that aspect of celebrations, but the ceremonial nature of this one meant it was difficult to avoid some level of introspection. When I look back on it, I think it's the first time I truly started to consider my football mortality.

After my interview and the presentation, the North Melbourne players formed a guard of honour, which meant a lot. Brett Ratten was their coach at the time. I messaged him after the game to pass on my thanks to the players for waiting around after a loss, even though it wasn't a traditional milestone. They had to stand on the field all through my TV commitments and the ceremony. I know that waiting around on the field after a loss is the last thing you feel like doing, so I appreciated them going through that.

It felt like a full-circle moment with Rats, who was standing in as senior coach while Alastair Clarkson was on leave. Rats was the coach who had given me my debut game and who was so encouraging of my journey, and now he was there again 12 years later to see me break a nearly 30-year record. It was nice to be able to share that with him.

Before the match I'd agreed to be miked up by the broadcaster Channel 7, and our conversation featured in the broadcast. Rats as always was a gentleman, complimenting me on what I'd achieved – what I'd done for my family and my people.

'You're the one that gave me my shot, so I appreciate it, I really appreciate it,' I said in return.

Initially, I didn't want the conversation to be broadcast by the club. I feel like not everything has to be public and maybe that should have been a private moment for us. But, in the end, I decided that Rats should be acknowledged for what he did for me when I was at Carlton.

I'd won a Premiership and now I'd surpassed Jim's record.

If someone had told me when I started, that my 'experiment' would be so successful, I wouldn't have believed them.

While I titled this book *The Irish Experiment*, my greatest hope for Gaelic football players who travel down under to transition to AFL is that they are no longer considered an 'experiment'.

From Jim Stynes' and Sean Wight's recruitment to

Melbourne Football Club to Mark O'Connor and me winning a Premiership, I think we can all agree that Gaelic footballers are perfectly primed to play Australian Rules football. Wight was recruited after he answered a newspaper ad looking for players for the 'Irish experiment'. He played minor football for Kerry, making it to the 1982 All-Ireland final. He moved to Australia in 1983 to play with the Melbourne Demons and is officially the first Gaelic footballer to sign with an AFL team. It's incredible to think that in 2022 two players out of the squad of 23 that won the Premiership were Irish – that's nearly 10 per cent of players on that day. In 2024, Conor McKenna became the fourth Irish player to win a flag when he won with the Brisbane Lions.

To give you another example, in round two in 2024, there were four Irish players on the field at the Adelaide Oval: Oisín Mullin, Mark O'Connor and me, representing Geelong, and Mark Keane wearing the Crows colours. The best part was that it wasn't even a big deal. I'm not sure it even rated a mention. That's when you know you're doing well: when you're known as a good footballer rather than 'the Irish player'.

That's not to say we mind the 'Irish experiment' label. I feel like it's developed into an affectionate term, and it's why I've chosen that title for this book.

Things have improved a lot for Irish recruits in the AFL since I started. Back when I was at Carlton, I wasn't even entitled to the moving allowance that was given to interstate players. These days, international players who move to Australia to play in the AFL or AFLW (the women's competition) are entitled to a relocation allowance of up to $16,500. In general, the health and welfare of players is much more of a priority. That means there is much better support in place for players who are struggling with the transition or with homesickness.

The future is bright for potential Irish recruits. With a nineteenth team – the Tasmania Devils – joining the competition in 2027, the number of players required will increase, so there'll be more opportunities. At some point, I'd like to be involved in helping Irish players make the most of that. I look back to the draft combine I did in Limerick and I know I'd like to facilitate that for young Irish players. I'm passionate about athletes getting the opportunity to be professional, if that's their goal. And the reality is, the GAA is never turning professional.

In GAA, you play for the love of the game. Believe me, I know – I couldn't love it more. But you can't lodge love of the game in your bank account, and I can assure you that it doesn't help secure a mortgage, or pay one off for that matter. Realistically, for Gaelic footballers who want sport to be their livelihood, the AFL is the best option. If you're not a professional soccer player by the time you're 15, it's not going to happen for you in that sport. And it happens for very few.

Because the modern Gaelic footballer doesn't get paid, they're referred to as 'amateur', but they train just as hard as AFL players. I know this for a fact, as I went to watch Laois train when I was back home for my wedding.

I wasn't the only visitor from the Cattery that day. My teammate Rhys Stanley and our assistant coach Nigel Lappin came along too. It was a wet, muddy evening at the Centre of Excellence in Portlaoise. The weather was damp but the energy was high, and we were all struck by the intensity of the session.

Gaelic football requires a different skill set, and the training reflected that. The sport is end-to-end because there are so few stoppages. Players train for that, for the ball to constantly be live. Everything they did at Laois training was high speed and one-on-one. I remember thinking there was no way my hamstrings would get through it. And these guys are training at this level after a full day at work or university. That's the part that Rhys and Nigel couldn't process – that this was an after-work activity. How they manage recovery from each session, never mind adequate sleep to maintain it, is beyond me. Luckily, I've never had to know.

Don't get me wrong, in an ideal world every Irish player that was approached to play AFL would say no, because they'd be treated so well by the GAA and their career would have become a viable way to pay the bills. I don't know what the answer is – the 'amateur' status of the GAA is sacrosanct

– but the reality is that players aren't training like amateurs anymore. For there to be limited reward for that – other than in bigger counties like Dublin that have sponsorship benefits and resources beyond the others – is crazy. The level of training can't keep trending upwards while the compensation (usually limited to food and mileage) remains the same.

What annoys me even more than the lack of compensation for players who dedicate their lives to the GAA, and in some cases fill Croke Park with paying customers, are those who criticise players for leaving.

Former Tyrone coach Mickey Harte was a vocal critic of the 'Irish experiment'. Then, when Kerry star David Clifford was on the radar of Australian scouts in 2017, there were plenty queuing up to have their say.

One was former Kerry player Tomás Ó Sé. He wrote a column talking about how the recruitment – or, in Clifford's case, attempted recruitment – of Irish players was 'just plain wrong'. He said counties in Ireland had 'zero protection against Australian clubs coming over here and cherry-picking our best young players'. He went on to say he wanted players to stay at home and 'follow their dreams' in Kerry, and not 'on the other side of the planet'. And just in case Mark O'Connor wasn't clear on how the locals felt about his departure from Kerry to Geelong, Ó Sé added: 'There are people in Dingle heartbroken that Mark O'Connor is gone.'

But what if the player's dream is to play sport for a living? How do they do that in Kerry? Sure, they might get a 'job' from a sponsor that requires little involvement so they can focus on training, but how many players does that happen for? And in how many counties does it happen? Kerry is a superpower and has the resources to match. It doesn't happen in counties like Laois.

It's funny how, when a player leaves GAA to play rugby, there aren't any such columns. None of the commentators seem to care. In fact, these players often get complimented on the increased skill level that their Gaelic football background has brought to rugby. But a player going to Australia to play Australian Rules? That automatically means the AFL is evil. They've taken an Irish player away from the love of the game to a weekly pay cheque.

And don't get me started on golf. Shane Lowry played Gaelic football for Clara, then left to tour the world as a professional golfer. How dare he? His dad Brendan, along with Shane's two uncles, won an All-Ireland with Offaly in 1982. With that pedigree, how could he leave Gaelic football? I haven't been able to find Tomás' article critiquing Shane Lowry for leaving or lamenting Clara's inability to protect their players from the invading forces of the PGA Tour, but I'm sure it's out there somewhere.

Why is AFL an evil code you can't give in to, but everything else is fine?

In case you haven't picked up on it, I have a serious issue

with anyone who dares to block an opportunity for a young player.

While the International Rules Series was partially blamed for the recruitment of Irish players, the main reason it ceased to exist after 2017 was the on-field fighting. For a few years, it was out of control.

It's a shame it was judged at a time when 'the biff' (fighting) was almost an accepted part of the game. These days, you cannot touch anyone in the AFL. I mean, punching someone in the face just doesn't happen anymore. While suspensions that affected the regular season were never introduced during the series, I know that the current regime wouldn't put up with what happened back then. I genuinely think the fights would be a thing of the past if it were to return. Both codes have matured so much in the past few years and, as we continue to learn more and more about the long-term effects of concussion, it's fair to say that the sort of behaviour that marred the series has been eliminated from the game.

Also, what about going back to the good old days when the opposing teams socialised? Organise a function where both teams go for a night out together and I guarantee we'll all end up best mates. It's not difficult to arrange.

These two indigenous codes will never have world cups, but they have a shared history that makes it worth reinstating the series, for both the men's and the women's code. Why not give these players the chance to represent their countries? It'd be an opportunity afforded to the All-Australian team, and if players weren't available to play and/or travel, then former All-Australians would be offered a place. It's important that the series is the best versus the best and that the standard is high. From an Irish point of view, that means it would be that year's All-Star team, or a former All-Star stepping in to replace players who weren't available.

People talk about the ball being a massive disadvantage for the Australians – and it's true, it takes time for them to adapt to the round ball. But the Aussies have their full-bodied tackle, which definitely takes time for Irish players to adapt to. When I played, I noticed how quickly my Irish teammates developed that skill. In the second match, there was always a noticeable improvement in their 360-degree awareness. With two groups of players so highly skilled in their individual codes, such a quick adoption of new rules is not a surprise.

So, let's bring it back. I'd love to play for Ireland again, and I hope the AFL and the GAA can make it happen.

As for golf? I would warn the GAA against any form of collaboration. We don't want to put our players in too many shop windows, now, do we?

CHAPTER 11

Leave It Before
It Leaves You

AT THE END OF THE 2023 SEASON, I RE-SIGNED with the Cats for another year, but not before seeking some reassurance from Chris Scott.

'I only want to play on next year if I can really contribute,' I said when I walked into his office. 'I don't want to be that player that stays on too long. The moment I don't think I can improve the team is the moment I'm going to step away.'

Chris has always been upfront with me, which I've appreciated. He told me I was part of his plans, as was the strategy to manage senior players regularly to ensure we peaked at the end of the season. He probably told me that because he knew I hadn't always been a fan of being 'managed'. He needed me to start being okay with it.

I appreciated his directness but in the off-season, I was met with a familiar low feeling. Perhaps it was the fact that we had missed out on finals just a year after winning the Premiership – I mean, it was the first time since I arrived at the Cattery that we hadn't played in September. Or maybe the high of surpassing Jim Stynes' milestone was being followed by an inevitable low. My playing days were numbered, and I knew it. Would 2024 be my last season?

I was now really considering my football mortality. There was no sweeping it under the carpet any longer.

With the feelings of melancholy came a familiar pattern, the pattern I had followed whenever things got tough.

I've always liked training on my own in the off-season. I genuinely look forward to working hard and devising plans that would help me maximise my performance in the coming year. I also think solo training has major benefits. Hitting your times is harder, and doing every session when there isn't anyone there to keep you accountable is mentally challenging – as is doing every rep and never cutting any corners. If you're tough enough to do everything when nobody's looking, you know you're going to find group training sessions significantly easier when you return.

But my 2023 off-season approach was less about the benefits and more about the fact that I just didn't want to be around my teammates. I started to develop this me-versus-the-world mentality and with that came a self-imposed exile from the group. I was actively avoiding them. If I knew they were planning to be at the Deakin University running track at 7 a.m. to do a session, I'd get there at 6 a.m., maybe even 5.30 a.m., just to make sure there was no chance of bumping into anyone. My teammates hadn't done anything wrong, I was just out of sorts and needed time on my own to process the season gone by – and what lay ahead.

Because of my preoccupation with how my future might look like post-AFL, I thought it would be a good idea to start putting things in place, in case it was my final year. Top of my to-do list was to organise a keynote speech, something I could present to sports teams or schools, or even in a corporate environment. But for that, I would need help.

I asked the player-welfare department if they knew who would be best to help. Of course they did. That's why Geelong is so good – they always have the right person to support you, whatever you need. They introduced me to a club consultant, Anna Box. Her PowerPoint skills were excellent, apparently.

I had met Anna before, but only very briefly. We met again in the café of the club and, as promised, she was great. She helped me piece together my presentation. And she was easy to talk to. Suspiciously easy.

I told her that I was starting to write my memoir, to be

released whenever I eventually retired. My presentation would reflect this very book's contents, but I was unsure exactly how to put it all together or what the themes might be.

She asked what was in the book. What would people learn about me?

Then I just started talking, about everything – from the year Flynn was born to moving clubs to thinking about the future. It felt like I was talking a lot, and about stuff I'd never talked about before. She was asking all the right questions and I felt like I had been talking for a long time.

'Are you a psychologist?' I ventured.

She smiled. 'Yes.'

I felt tricked, in a good way. She'd tricked me into the therapy I'd always needed, the chat I'd never had. She was like a therapy ninja who had ambushed me.

I told her that the main theme I wanted to lean into was how terribly I'd handled adversity – withdrawing from everyone and just struggling through it alone. I wanted to make sure my kids didn't grow up to be like me, in that regard.

Then she said something no one had ever said before. 'What makes you think you handled it terribly? I mean, it worked out, didn't it? You got through it, and a lot of people don't.'

'Shit, I hadn't thought about it like that before,' I said.

Did I do okay? Surely not.

But she was right. I did get through it, and, for the most part, things were really good now.

What I found out that day was that everything was okay.

For anyone who fears having those conversations, go and do it. The right person will make you feel better. Sometimes, it takes an outsider to point out the obvious.

With a new perspective and a clear head, it was time to focus on 2024. I returned to group training shortly afterwards and was delighted to be reunited with my teammates. Some had been abroad doing their solo training, others had stuck around and formed a small running club. We were all back together. It was time to look ahead to 2024.

If it was going to be my last season, then so be it. I was going to make it a good one.

Our season got off to a flyer. We won seven in a row. We were surprising everyone, including ourselves.

I've mentioned how many Irish players were on the field for our round two win over the Adelaide Crows, but even more significant was the 150th-match milestone of my good friend Tom Stewart. Being chaired off doesn't usually happen until you reach 200 games but, in Tom's case, it was a unanimous decision that it had to be done. He's won five All-Australians in his career and he's also one of the best blokes you could ever meet. Getting a win to mark this achievement was special. Celebrating the milestones of your good friends is one of the joys of playing the game, and they do it really well in Geelong.

Because of our results, Chris was able to start managing the senior players early. He told me that he wanted me to have one week off in the first four, and he'd prefer it if I was available to take on the Western Bulldogs in round four rather than playing Hawthorn in round three. I knew it was the plan and I took it well.

To say I've become better at these conversations is an understatement. At one point during the pandemic in 2020, we played five games in 19 days and my knee blew up. I'd been managing the knee injury that saw me miss the start of the 2019 season, and it had been going well generally, but this condensed streak of games caused it to become severely inflamed and it needed draining.

Ever wondered what the fluid that gets drained from your knee looks like? Apple juice. Not the cloudy type, but the clearer apple juice that's cheaper at the supermarket. I don't know if you needed that visual, but you have it now. You're welcome.

Anyway, I needed that apple juice out of my knee and our team doctor Drew Slimmon informed me I wouldn't be playing the following week. It was a reasonable prognosis as I could barely walk at that point.

So what did I do when he gave me this information? I grabbed a white plastic garden chair that was sitting innocently on the sideline and chucked it at him. Don't worry, the chair was fine – and so was the doctor. I had enough self-control to deliberately miss, but maybe not by as much as I should have. So, yeah, didn't take it great. Sorry, Doc.

Anyway, the point of this 2020 flashback is to demonstrate just how far I had progressed when it came to receiving the news that I wasn't playing – or, in 2024 terminology, that I was 'being managed'. No garden chairs were harmed when Chris Scott told me I would be rested in round three, or round six for that matter.

When I returned in round seven to take on Carlton, I was feeling good thanks to the week off. So much so that for just the third time in my career, I kicked three goals. This was my first hat-trick for Geelong and my first in a victory. My previous two three-goal hauls had occurred when I was playing for Carlton in losses. No one pats you on the back for a hat-trick when you've lost. Thanks to a 13-point win, my three goals was a good-news story and a sign Geelong's 'management' strategy was working.

Everything was going well: it was our seventh consecutive win. Then we hit a slump.

We lost six out of the next seven matches, including a 64-point thrashing at the hands of the Gold Coast Suns in Darwin.

Now, you'd think that would result in a change of attitude or strategy from Scotty. Not at all. He stuck by his plan – doubled down, even. There was no change to the schedule. Our diary at Geelong always offers a good work–life balance, and it didn't change. Scotty never pointed the finger at anyone, ever. He never has. I don't think he has it in him.

Eventually, we emerged from our losing streak to win three-in-a-row and move to third on the ladder. That's where we finished the season – top four again. A year after missing out altogether.

The closer we got to September, the more the decision about my future weighed on me. I had been quietly mulling over it for most of the year but, in the build-up to our round 22 clash with Fremantle, I knew I had to make a call either way, and one thought in particular had been forefront in my mind: the prospect of my 300-game milestone.

If I played on, I could reach that enticing number. What an achievement it would be. How good would it look on my CV? The more this thought featured on my list of reasons to keep going, the more I decided it was a major red flag. The day you are mainly motivated by personal achievement or an individual milestone is the day you need to give it up. Sure, it would be nice, but playing on for that reason would be selfish.

I bumped into our head of development, former assistant coach Nigel Lappin.

'Can we catch up?' I asked. 'There's some stuff I need to

talk to you about.' Nigel and I are really close, so my asking for a meeting rather than just dropping in meant he knew it was serious. 'I need to run some thoughts I have by you … about retirement.'

He agreed straightaway. I could tell that he knew I was gone. Nige is one of very few people I trust unequivocally to always give me honest feedback, and not just on footy matters but everything.

When we caught up, I told him about my fears of playing one year too long (so many players end up regretting it) and that I only wanted to continue if I could keep improving, that I couldn't cope with anything less. I think he knew the decision had been made. Nige told me about his retirement and what he'd been thinking at the time. Turned out, he had gone through the exact same thought process.

I needed guidance and, as always, Nige delivered. I knew he would. I didn't say anything at the end of the meeting. I just said I'd let him know.

I already knew.

As soon as I walked out of his office, I called Bec. She was driving at the time.

'I'm pretty sure I'm retiring,' I said.

There was silence for a moment, then I heard an audible gasp on the other end of the line. She was aware I was thinking about it, but the finality of knowing it, and maybe not expecting the decision on this particular day, had shocked her.

I told my parents over the phone. They told me how proud they were of me. Their tone was tinged with relief. They knew what a big decision it was, and they were happy that I was content and confident it was the right time.

Then, I put the news on the family WhatsApp for my siblings. There were a lot of people to tell, and this approach saved me time.

The following day, I confirmed with Nigel Lappin before telling our assistant coach James Kelly, discreetly, during training.

When that was done, I went into Chris Scott's office.

'This doesn't have to be a long chat. I just wanted to let you know I'm done at the end of the year,' I said.

I said it didn't have to be a long chat because I didn't want it to be a long chat. I knew it could become emotional for me and I didn't want to put him in that situation. We still had a job to do. We were at the business end of the season.

'We'll catch up another time and discuss it,' he said. 'We don't need to talk about it now.'

I was in and out of his office in about four minutes.

Having told everyone I needed to tell, I decided I would now ride off into the sunset. I wouldn't be saying anything publicly or even to my teammates. I just wouldn't be there when pre-season started. Eventually, I was persuaded that approach would be counterproductive. Nigel Lappin, James Kelly and our player-development manager Mark Worthington all pointed out that I would be asked questions by media throughout finals and that it could become distracting.

In the build-up to our last home game for the season at GMHBA Stadium – against the West Coast Eagles – I stood up in a team meeting and addressed the group.

Not even some of my closest friends on the team knew about my decision before I began to speak but, as soon as I stood up, they could tell what was about to happen. If a senior player stands up to talk in a team meeting, it can only mean one thing.

I'd prepared my speech diligently the night before. I started writing it after dinner and, hours later, I woke Bec up to ask her to come out to the living room and hear the final product. It was after 11 p.m., and I'd written down my thoughts on four A4 pieces of paper. She was happy with it, and so was I.

When delivering it, what helped the most was having the paper to look at. I had rehearsed it and knew what I needed to say – I didn't need the paper as a prompt – but what I did need was to get through it without getting emotional. What do you need to avoid when you're controlling your emotions? Eye contact. Eye contact is your enemy in these situations.

The acknowledgements at the end of this book were formed from the basis of my speech. Because it included everyone I needed to thank, for everything.

My last match at GMHBA turned out to be the fairytale

farewell. In the build-up, I asked my son Flynn how I should celebrate if I kicked a goal. He suggested I make a heart shape with my fingers. We practised it together and I was ready to go. I honestly didn't think I'd get to use it – I mean, that would be too perfect.

Lo and behold, in the third quarter, I got the chance to kick a goal.

Actually, that's not accurate. Brad Close was paid a free kick – it was his – but I chose to play on. I definitely shouldn't have, but I just thought, *Fuck it.* I was desperate for a goal. And I got one.

Then, I did it. The heart shape was meant for my family: I knew where Bec, Flynn and Rafferty were sitting and I aimed it in their direction. The crowd cheered, as they had been cheering every kick of mine throughout the game. As always, Geelong supporters showed me love that I couldn't have dreamed of before I arrived at the club. I'd had no idea just how much they would accept me and support me. How lucky had I been to come to this town, to this club?

In that moment, I realised the heart couldn't just be for my immediate family; it needed to be for my Geelong family too. I pirouetted around to show them the love. Who knew Flynn's idea for a celebration would end up being my official thank you to Geelong?

We beat the West Coast Eagles by 93 points. Brad Close told me after the game that if anyone else had played on and tried to kick a goal off his free kick, he'd have been pissed off. But, given the occasion, he was glad to have contributed to the heart moment.

Because we finished third on the ladder, we had to travel over to Adelaide to play Port Adelaide in our qualifying final in week one of finals. As usual, we were assembled in the meeting room on the Thursday before the game to go through the team lineup. I was in the room already when I got a text from Scotty to ask me to come outside.

'You're going to be the sub this week,' he said. 'I didn't want you to find out by seeing it on the board.'

I appreciated him telling me. This was not a good time of year for it to happen, but I understood he had to make those decisions. It occurred to me pretty early on that playing my way out of the sub's role would not be easy.

That challenge increased when we smashed Port by 84 points to book our spot in the preliminary final. It's always difficult to lose the sub tag but when your side wins that well and you've only been subbed on after the game is already decided, it's close to impossible.

I was left out of the side to play the Brisbane Lions in the preliminary final. It was tough to take. But, as always, I respected Scotty's decision. I'm pretty sure he didn't enjoy making the call either as, to be fair, we've always had a great relationship. But with an eye towards having another crack at a flag, he made what he thought was the right decision. I respect him greatly for that.

Scotty's ability to consistently put his players in a position to succeed is what I admire most about him. He could have taken the easy route and bottomed out for a few years, as so many other clubs do, but that's not in his make-up. Every year, he looks his players dead in the eye and says, 'I'll go all-in, if you will.' This approach doesn't guarantee you'll win anything, but it gives you a chance, and that's all I've ever wanted. A chance.

He is, by far, the best senior coach I've had in my career. It's been an absolute honour and a privilege to be coached by Chris Scott.

I watched the preliminary final with Bec, Flynn and Rafferty, and the other players who weren't in the match-day squad. Cats legend Tom Hawkins, who had also announced his retirement, was sitting a few rows in front of me.

It was agonising to watch. We held a 25-point lead in the third quarter but, all of a sudden, the momentum changed. I could see the Lions had lifted and, watching as a spectator, there was nothing I could do. We ended up losing by 10 points.

The season was over. My career was over.

When the final siren sounded, I sat with my head in my hands for what felt like a couple of minutes. I could feel friends patting me on the back, trying to offer reassurance.

Part of me couldn't believe it; part of me was so grateful to all the Geelong fans who had come up to wish me well and thank me.

It was a strange way for it to end. But in sport, you don't get to choose your exact ending. I'd had my goodbye in Geelong. The preliminary final wasn't meant to turn out this way, but it had.

In that moment, I just had to think about 20-year-old me. The newly arrived Gaelic footballer who was in his first season with Carlton, playing in the VFL, only to be dropped to the VFL reserves. If someone had said to me back then, 'Not to worry, you'll end up with 288 games – a record for an Irish player – and a Premiership', would I have taken that outcome? You bet I would!

A few days later, we went on our 'Wacky Wednesday'. A group of us from the club's chess club dressed up as chess pieces. I went as a bishop. And yes, you heard me right, I set up a chess club at the Cattery. I'm hopeful that it will be part of my lasting legacy.

In the weeks since making my decision, a comment from former Liverpool legend Jamie Carragher has really stuck with me. While critiquing Brazilian midfielder Casemiro's performances for Manchester United, he quipped that it's important to 'leave the football before the football leaves you'.

Carragher's been criticised for daring to suggest that the five-time Champions League winner should 'leave the football', but what he said really resonated with me. It's a decision that every athlete is forced to make one day, and it's an important one.

That's what I did. I left Australian Rules football before it left me. More than anything, I'll forever be grateful that Australian Rules found me in the first place. I've spent my entire adult life in this game, and it's given me so much. I just hope I made a few people smile along the way.

Thank you for everything.
I love you all.

PS: C'mon the Town – see you soon.

Acknowledgements

I was 17 when I was first spotted by an AFL scout.

I was 19 when I moved to Australia permanently.

I was 21 when I made my AFL debut and, on the day I turned 22, I met the woman who would eventually become my wife.

I was 24 when my first son was born.

I was 26 when I joined the Cats.

I was 29 when my second son was born.

I was 32 when I was part of a Premiership team, and later that same year I got married.

That's it. That's everything: my crowning achievements. The only problem is, they are not actually *my* achievements.

The 17-year-old wouldn't have been spotted if he didn't have parents who drove him the length and breadth of the country in pursuit of his sporting dreams.

The 21-year-old would never have debuted if he didn't have coaches who were prepared to invest countless hours into his development.

The 22-year-old would never have met his future wife if his best mate hadn't introduced him to her, and although I played a fairly key roll in the birth of our kids, I think it's fair to say Bec did most of the heavy lifting.

The 26-year-old was only allowed the privilege of joining the Cats because of the key decision-makers who saw fit to sign him, and God knows I played no more than a small part in our 2022 Premiership success.

That is my very long-winded way of saying that basically everything I've ever achieved is a direct result of the kindness and hard work of others. With that in mind, let me thank some people.

To my family and friends, thank you for everything. I can't imagine where I would be without you all.

To the Carlton Football Club, thank you. You certainly didn't have to give me a chance but you did. I'll forever be grateful to the Blues and all the Blue Baggers out there for their support over the journey.

To the Cats, you've given me more than I could have ever hoped for when I joined. Not least of all a Premiership. A bond I'll forever share with the club, and one that means the world to me.

To Catherine Murphy for the chats, the insights and everything you did to make this book what it is. Also to the team at Affirm Press for all the work they did to produce it and get it out into the world. And thanks to Hachette Ireland for everything on the Irish publication.

And finally to my wife, Bec, and my two sons, Flynn and Rafferty. You've ridden every bump along the way and been the support I needed. I love you all.